RETAIL JAIL
RETAIL APOCALYPSE

BOBBY DAZZLER

VANCOUVER BC

Retail Jail: Retail Apocalypse
© Jasbir Rai, 2018

ISBN: 978-1-988368-04-7

Cover Design by Diane Feught

Prepared for Bobby Dazzler by Alpha Glyph Publications
Vancouver, BC, Canada

www.bobbydazzler.ca

Resources: The Vancouver Sun, Goggle Baba and other online searches

Retail Jail

Retail Apocalypse

Contents

Bobby Dazzler

According to the dictionary, Bobby Dazzler means a person or thing that is outstanding or excellent.

- Anything outstanding, striking or showy, especially an attractive girl

At the time of inception, the name was chosen by a marketing company who thought it would be catchy, appropriate and memorable for a retail business. The name was meant to reflect and apply to all the things that the store sold. It was a name that stuck with people and resonated with the British, Scottish, Aussies down South, and North Americans. It had a certain sex appeal! Since the name was used for the store, then it was natural to write about Bobby Dazzler, while being Bobby Dazzler. After all, clients, suppliers and other businesses would always call up the store asking to speak to Bobby Dazzler. Being the owner of the store, it was easy to say, "Speaking." As time goes on, you become what you are. So, the owner became Bobby Dazzler, literally! The name has been trademarked in Canada.

Intro

After retailing for nearly 30 years, Bobby Dazzler had some interesting stories to share with people. Being born, raised, and educated in Canada, it was a dream to be an entrepreneur in the retail world. Especially for a Indian girl born to immigrant parents who wanted their child to be a doctor or lawyer. It was one of the highest personal feats to reach for a 70's kid. Retail is creative, exciting and different from the norms that most people go by. Sure, it is hard, challenging and very easy to fail in, just like many other businesses. However, it appeared that retail was a true calling in a certain special way that led to so many other aspects of life being fulfilled. It is the love for sales! The love of a business! The love for people! Working for yourself has many benefits! Learning from the many people that walked into the store made retailing all the more exciting. Plus, it is fun to create a retail store with products that were hand picked, put together so that a concept could be created from nothing. Bobby Dazzler was that concept! What began as a means of making money and a livelihood for the family, later turned out be an exciting place where so many other events in life took place. It was indeed the first love for so, so many years until it eventually became a retail jail where the passion for it finally died.

That passion started to dwindle along with the other retailers who were part of a retail apocalypse that began in 2008 in the United States and some parts of Canada. The poor sales just never picked up to pre-2008 levels. The poor sales only multiplied to a low in late 2016 and right into the entire 2017 onwards. Retailers were hurting and were part of a shift that consumers were going through. Retailing is truly part of the materialistic world. Everything brand name was looked upon as cool until people just started to wake up to a whole new world. Humans had taken the simplest thing: water, and decided to put it into plastic bottles with funky labels and brands to sell it for a profit. Retailing and the materialistic world had gone too far. People were starting to mature and get wiser. It appeared that ethical consumerism was starting to take off. That is when retailing also started to take a nosedive. Society was not as naïve and gullible to the whole idea of "let's just buy it!" People were becoming conscious of what they did with their hard-earned money. Consumers were no longer just dropping money on just about anything without a reason. Over time, Bobby Dazzler took notice of all the different changes that were taking place in the retail world. These changes will be discussed in *Retail Apocalypse* along with some technical points on the "how to" of retail.

As things rolled daily in the Bobby Dazzler store, observation led to a documentation of what was actually happening. The hours in the mall got longer and longer along with the number of the days the mall was closed during the year. Then, there were personal events that made retailing difficult which included a certain amount of harassment and being unable to renew a lease in the most profitable store location. As time went on, the retail world started to feel like a jail due to the changing dynamics of retail. That is how the story of *Retail Jail - Retail Apocalypse* came to be. It so happened chapters of the book ended up being five letters each. This is interesting, since it is a fact that 555 in numerology denotes major shifts and spiritual growth. Perhaps this retail apocalypse appears to be a catalyst for people to experience a whole new world: a world with less retail and consumerism, and more experiences closer to spirituality. This shift took on a whole new momentum by late 2016 and beyond. Bobby Dazzler's lease was to expire by mid-2017 and the time had come to be released from the retail jail to bring forth a new world. There were many different issues and problems that had been experienced by Bobby Dazzler over the years. Some of the problems and issues were normal retailer problems that were general and could prove to be helpful for an individual deciding to go into retail. However, others were personal and specific to Bobby Dazzler. This book will discuss both the general and personal challenges of retailing in a "reveal all". Sure, there were positive experiences in retailing as no one would stay in retailing for nearly 30 years if it wasn't fun and profitable. But the fun dried up towards the end. Retail hours, retail sales, retail rents and the passion for retail going from really high to really low made it feel as if it were a prison. Hence, the term "retail jail".

On a positive note, there are many different secrets revealed in order to be a successful retailer. There are important topics that can help a retailer who is just emerging and also help those who are already retailing. Writing enables a healing process but this healing can also be revealing of all. There are many reasons that retail can be termed as a jail but the ones that are personal to this story truly made it a sort of prison that cannot be described by others in the same way. There were shady characters, events and issues that were connected to the retail business that made this story a unique experience to be shared with others. Yes, this can happen to a little retailer.

START

Nobody wakes up one day and says, I am going to start a retail business. It is just something that starts with the love of people. Like all businesses, the retail business is difficult to start. Dealing with the general public day in and day out is very difficult if people are not your thing. So, the core of the business is the love of service to the people. Customer service is based on treating all people the same. The best place to start a retail business is first asking yourself if a genuine care of people exists. Sure, it helps to have business in the blood through family. But by the age of 15, after helping family incorporate a business and seeing the fruits of self-employment, it was not even a question that business was it.

After working for large corporations like Revenue Canada, Western Cable systems and summer stints at fish factories cutting fish, some money was saved but not enough to start a business. Capital or money is definitely needed to start a retail business or any business for that matter. Obtaining financing at the age of 19 is often difficult, especially from banks. It might even be really difficult to ask family for $250K when there is no experience in business yet. After wishing for some good luck, Bobby Dazzler eventually got a break Getting into retail by 19 going on 20 while attending university is difficult. No bank lends money to a teen without any strong finances. Going to daddy was out of the question since he thought that it is best to work for large companies to reap the rewards of medical benefits and retirement plans. However, after working for large corporations, it easy to see why people got sick and looked forward to retirement. The happiness level appeared to be lower than the idea of working for the self. A happy person tends not to get sick often and doesn't look forward to retirement when they actually enjoy what they do. Everyday becomes a holiday if you're making money. Self-employment was a good place to be happy as it provided for different rewards than company benefits like a dental, medical or retirement plan. After all, if you love what you do, then you are less likely to get sick or have a desire to retire.

So, after being the top business/accounting student for two years straight in high school and obtaining a couple of small scholarships, the business world was definitely the top choice. High school provided courses like Accounting, Law, Economics, Advanced Accounting, Typing and Computer Sciences to help get a good start in business. There was a strong interest in this field and it is a great base to have if a retail business was going to be the way. Going to Simon Fraser University and pursuing a Liberal Arts education was actually more rewarding than pursuing the number-crunching Finance, Economics and Accounting courses. Psychology seemed much more helpful to sales and marketing than knowing all the number-crunching. After all, if we could figure out how people work then it would be easier to sell to them and become successful. The retail store was opened at the same time as going to school part-time. So the focus was on school and business only. There was no time for socialization with so much money being invested in a business. Thus, a really strong grasp of the business world was already in place by 19. It took six years to complete the BA degree in Liberal Arts/Psychology and a Minor in Business. However, the retail experience of running a retail store provided much more experience than school ever did as it was hands-on, relevant and for real. The schooling was hypothetical only. Choosing to go to the store was always favored instead of going to SFU and that is why it took six years to do a four-year degree. The Bobby Dazzler business came before anything else did, even school. There was even a time when the final exam for Economics 333 was skipped on December 19th in 1995. This was because December 19 is one of the busiest days of the year and there was no way it could be left for others to run when sales would easily reach $25K on that day based on the past years' sales. That course was so difficult, it could be repeated and there was no way I could focus on it knowing that the store was jam-packed with people, sales, money and profit.

Being self-employed, self-reliant and self-sufficient got to be more and more attractive as time went on. It seemed like a really attractive way to earn a living and be free. So the original purpose of going into business was for personal fulfillment. However, the success of it brought immense materialistic success. It provided money for a house, a car, a livelihood and other nice things but ultimately it was the freedom to be "your own boss".

Back to how the store was financed without going to a bank or going to the parents. After graduation in 1989, friends would go to the Rodeo Drive of Vancouver and cruise with their cars. One night while cruising, a red Jaguar pulled over with three guys who asked my two friends and me if we wanted to hang out with them for ice cream. Yah, right? Ice Cream, huh? We all took a chance and agreed to cruising around with them and meeting up. I mean what's not fun riding around in a Jaguar in Vancouver at the age of 17? We all became friends and some of us started to date. The business plan was being written at that time and projections were being constructed. Capital was needed to start the retail business and the required amount was to the tune of $125K. One of the individuals in the Jaguar was named Major. After giving him a basic plan, he ended up providing the additional financing necessary to start up the Bobby Dazzler store in October 1990 which was the following year. That was fast, right? Well sometimes, we to have to take risks and chances. That is what business is all about. Making connections and hoping that the right person shows up at the right time. It was a loan that would be needed to be repaid back in two-three years with interest. Major and I parted ways upon repayment of the loan. He was not interested in the long hours and number of days that retail was open. The business was fully taken over 100% upon payment of the loan. Bobby Dazzler belonged to the current owner and writer of the book 100% from that time onwards.

Sure, it was challenging in the beginning being an Indo-Canadian woman owning her own business by the early age of 23. Mom and Dad thought Bobby Dazzler was going to a Sari store or a 24K Gold jewelry store business. Anything but a novelty store that sold knick-knacks, party stuff, gadgets and gizmos. It was just really a different retail store from the rest. It had to be a store like that.

Like many other businesses, Bobby Dazzler ran into problems in the start of the business back in the early years due to it being far too high end for the likes of the general, local Vancouver consumers. Market trends and product requests were geared towards the $20 range of products. It did not take long for Bobby Dazzler to understand that if we didn't change our ways to a less expensive, novelty-based and a low/mid-priced product, then we could jeopardize losing the store and the concept. The start could easily have been the end if we didn't tweak the business model to meet the consumer demands. We were a "mom-pop" type of outlet that was able to change our ways quickly to accommodate the market . That is probably why a retailer like us was able to last almost 30 years. Otherwise, we too could have gone up in smoke like Target (Canada) after just two years of starting in Canada.

BOBBY

There are large and small stores around the world that are fueling this whole notion that humanity needs more and more stuff. Bobby Dazzler was no different since we were just a small retailer that might have joined in the whole hoarding movement of the materialism age. But at least there was something to share with humanity, since the store survived so many years of retailing. Our store had certain items that were basically wants rather than needs. It was fun stuff and stuff that nobody really needed but wanted.

Having a store means that you have accepted to enter the world of materialism. After all, retail is all about selling items or more stuff. It was novelty retail. Novelty is fun one minute and boring the next day. Like all retail it is cut-throat and very competitive; just like the restaurant industry. It can be fickle but when you know what you are doing then it becomes easy and a template for future stores to be opened upon. When you get into the retail world, you realize that every Tom, Dick and Harry wants to get in on what you have but you've got it and it's hot. Bobby Dazzler always tried to stay ahead of the game. The store kept the items fresh and attempted to get items before other retailers got them.

But what does it mean to be a retailer that's "got it"? Having a store is both an art and science. One must be unique and innovative which was incidentally our motto for a number of years until it was time to rebrand the store and give it the motto, "got what's hot!" in 2005. Competition, department stores, online sales, sometimes grocery stores and even dollar stores encroaching our items and attempting to cash in on hot product meant that we were NO longer unique NOR innovative. If the store was going to survive, it needed to be constantly changing and updated with the types of items that were sold so that it would never appear stale. This was to ensure that the sales would always roll in. Paris Hilton started the trendy saying, "That's hot!" to just about everything that is hot. Bobby Dazzler became really hot and changed the business to cater to the hottest, newest trends! We went from unique and innovative gadgets, gifts and ideas to party, drinking, sex, smoking and a whole lot more hot stuff. It was just a waste to copy other stores or be like the department stores.

Bobby Dazzler needed to carve out its own niche. So it did and became:

Bobby Dazzler
"got what's hot!"

The store opened in October 1990 and actually made up to five stores and a kiosk at YVR. So it did become a multi-store operation at one point. The store was in a class of its own. Bobby Dazzler was unique, off the wall and very unusual. Often it would feel as if one had walked into a museum. Bobby Dazzler did exude a cross between being a night club in the day with a trance/rave party that is ongoing from the last night as soon as we opened. Our aura was just the same. We had bright pink and blue neon lights all around the store with flashing lights and loud music. It was important to appeal to the senses. It is not enough just having the right product but it is important to have the perfect ambience along with the "total product" experience for the client so that the store appealed to the senses. Everything around the product including the scent of the store, the music, the colors and the staff had to match the items that we sold. The staff was not the usual normal Joes either. They also seemed to be different each and every time. Only the unusual got hired and lasted. After all, only an unusual person would be able to sell unusual products in our store.

"Got what's hot!" was the motto and worked for a very long time until closure. We had it and got it first. The Bobby Dazzler store had a beautiful entrance to the world of retail. We were able to captivate the audience and catch them with the eye of appeal to the senses. Bobby Dazzler was a cool place to shop and even browse in. The store was able to dominate the mind of the consumer with our stuff. The store even looked busier than we were and the effect of the museum without the entrance fee was always there. Bobby Dazzler was energy and a draw to any of the malls that it was in. People were not able to simply walk by without taking a look. It was a shop like no other!

Ideas

Ideas are what make the world go around. Ideas shape society and allow for creativity, change and movement leading to exciting projects being launched. Retail concepts are created from ideas. Retail was having its heyday in the 80's and the 90's. So when Bobby Dazzler was coming to be in 1990, it was essentially being grown at a time when retail was enjoying great success. People were loving malls, stores and going shopping was more than just a pastime. The idea of going to the mall was a part of socialization for many people. Ideas that made shopping fun, exciting and pleasing to the senses made retailers even more successful. So the unique and innovative idea of creating a retail store that appealed to the senses back in 1990 was ahead of the game. It was futuristic and a visionary concept that would last. The idea was to create a store that many age groups could pop in and shop in. It was originally meant to appeal to the upper class but would eventually change with the times to appeal to all classes of people. The idea of Bobby Dazzler was to make gifts, gadgets and gizmos to those who had a lot of disposable income. The idea was naturally to buy low and sell as high as possible. However, after a couple of years of running the store, it was determined that most people did not fit into the category of buying mid to high priced gifts, gadgets or gizmos. It was a concept that was supposed to be loosely similar to the Sharper Image idea which was a wildly successful American retail/mail order concept that started in 1977 and eventually went bankrupt in 2008. It was later relaunched as an online and catalog business by Camelot Venture Group.

STUFF

"This is the kind of stuff that dreams are made out of" is the common saying in that you would never think, imagine nor feel that it's going to happen to you until it does. This kind of stuff only happens in the movies, I thought once to myself. But, as the Bobby Dazzler story goes along, it becomes unbelievable with stuff that went on in our little retail store.

Our store was on the cutting edge, we tended to carry stuff that was hot. Hot is what is trendy and what is "in". Items that were trending were found on the internet and people came asking for them after going shopping in the United States. The U.S. always had trendy items before the Canadian retailers got it. Stuff was hot if a celebrity was using the item. Hot items were YouTube sensations or a craze that everybody wants immediately after seeing it on television. People love to have what everybody else has. That is what hot stuff was. Our staff always loved to get the most interesting requests for stuff that was considered hot. The store would promptly take their name, their number and the request down. If we got enough people requesting the stuff, Bobby Dazzler would bring it in. This was another way to find out what was hot! We got asked so many ridiculous requests that we could actually honor most of them, and that is what made us hot retailers. Okay, in many sales training classes and in the retail world, we are all very aware that we are required to aim to please, not please to aim. How far do we go? What are the limits of the phrase? Is the customer always right? Where does the salesperson stop to think, is this even worth my while? Are we even going to get this back? Or better yet, did we even sell this item in our store? Yes, Bobby Dazzler did get many requests that were beyond outrageous but the stuff we had was out there and novel.

Some of the hot items that we carried were knick knacks that department stores didn't care about or to stock:
- Singing Bass Fish (Sang "don't worry be happy") - sold hundreds
- Laser Pointers
- Lava Lamps - always hot every single year
- Southpark Squeezies - sold thousands
- Minecraft Product - could not keep it in stock
- Playboy items - all products totally hot

- Superhero items - extremely popular 2013-2018
- Lighting products
- Novelty and Naughty t-shirts (that department stores find to risqué to carry)
- Bachelorette Party and Sex items
- Party items
- Smoking items
- Drinking items
- Superhero Stuff
- Massage products
- Novelty everything

Rules

Like many other things in life, retail has rules. Retail starts with creating a company. Generally, a business should incorporate through legal means to establish a limited company so that if liabilities occur only the company is exposed to them, not the individual owner of the business. Bobby Dazzler always incorporated. The incorporation of a company can be done by a lawyer or one is able to do this by oneself online. This incorporation is done Provincially in Canada. However, if the business is in the United States then different rules apply. These rules discussed here apply to those who retail in Canada. After a company is established, the rules require the business to present a business plan. The business plan outlines all the details of the retail concept along with financial information that enables a bank and/or a landlord to determine if they are interested in doing business with the retailer. Once it is established the retail concept is a go ahead, only then can proper financing be made available to open the business and to carry it on for at least a year or two if no profits arise right away. Financing can be acquired from banks or it can be done by individual business owners themselves through private means, namely through family or friends. Nevertheless, a sound financial plan leads to the successful operation of any retail business. So, part of the rules means following a plan properly and not wavering. Once financing is in place, a location is chosen. Normally this requires one to produce architectural plans or blueprints that are drawn up for approval by the landlord. Upon approval from the landlord, the plans are then submitted to the Municipal city to the various Permits departments for approval prior to construction. Permits are required before any type of demolition, renovation or construction can proceed. Some permits that are required in Canada are:

Building Permit
Electrical Permit
Plumbing Permit
Demolition Permit
Sprinkler Permit
Occupancy Permit
Security Alarm Permit

Food Permits (Health/Safety Permits)
Building Accessibility Permits for people with disabilities
Business Licenses
Fire Department permit
Tobacco Licenses (sales of cigarettes and vaporizers are regulated)

The above may seem like there are many permits and licenses that may be required but they are necessary when opening up for retail in order for compliance. Different sets of rules apply to those retailing the United States. The Government offices for permits and licensing can be located with a quick Google search in order to determine exactly which permits or licenses are required. These rules must be adhered to; otherwise there is no way a retailer is going to open for business. After all the permits are in place, the final approval from the landlord is still required to actually open for business. Nevertheless, plans must be approved according to the landlord's rules with respect to the operations of a store within their complex. So, rules must be approved in accordance with the city/municipality, the Province or State, in some cases with the Federal government and with the landlord. These seem like a lot of rules but they must be followed in order to get the retail business to open, especially in large malls. This is where Bobby Dazzler usually did its retail business. These steps can take some time and they are very, very stringent when it comes to getting approval based on the rules. A proper plan needs to be in place with coordination. After going through these two sets of approvals according to the rules, the retailer is able to build their store in the mall, strip mall or free-standing location within a specified time period that has been agreed upon in the lease during negotiations. If a store is unable to open in a timely manner, usually there are fines associated with delayed construction and renovation per day that a retail store is not open. They can become very, very expensive if the delays are long.

Upon completion of the renovation, the retailer moves to getting a business license and insurance to open for business officially. These rules must be followed since they are enshrined inside the legal document known as the lease that is signed by the retailer and the landlord. Those rules are usually iron-clad due to the strict lease that the landlord (owner) of the malls make all retailers sign when they rent space from the landlord. Those rules generally come in the form of clauses inside the lease. Inside those clauses are further rules, statutes, regulations, compliance rules and other laws that are governmental in nature at all the levels-municipal, provincial and federal. Not following one of the rules can cause the lease to be broken. The lease can be a long and very complicated document for the ordinary person to read and understand. The only time a lease is not signed is when a retailer owns the building and doesn't pay rent to a landlord. In this instance, rules of the city/municipality/town must still be adhered to. This however is very, very rare. Most retail complexes are leased by tenants and are not owned. Bobby Dazzler signed some leases that were up to 100 pages long for a 650 square foot space. If one is not a lawyer, the chances are the retailer will have almost no chance of fully understanding the wording and the technical jargon that are deeply embedded inside the lease. The wording in most cases is so difficult to comprehend that these rules sometimes can be broken easily by the retailer who hasn't understood all the clauses which are essentially the rules one must follow when conducting their retail business in a space leased from the landlord. Rules can sometimes be very exasperating and can cause the retailer to feel confined in a jail-like agreement when conducting business. This is even more true if the retail business is not doing well. This is where part of the *Retail Jail* title comes from. Yet without the lease, there is no business. This will be discussed further in the chapter *Lease*.

SALES

Sales in the retail world used to be special events. People used to wait for them and they were highly anticipated during certain times of the month or year. Some sales are really, really big such as Cyber Monday, Black Friday, or Boxing Day sales in Canada. In the past, retailers used to have traditional monthly sales, like Woodward's, a former retailer in Canada, who used to hold its "$1.49 day, Tuesday" sales monthly. However, as retailing got more and more competitive, intensified with more players and more saturation of retailers, it appeared that sales were no longer special events or occasions that needed to be waited for. There were sales monthly, weekly, daily, hourly and then 24/7 via cyberspace. Black Friday sales could be found in the summer, one day after Halloween or for the entire month of November. Sales lost their luster when they were always available. This definitely made retailing difficult for the bricks and mortar retailer. Profit margins got thinner and thinner with the number of sales going on all the time.

By May 2017, there were 3,742 strip malls and enclosed malls larger than 40,000 square feet in Canada alone. The United States had even more retail space than the Canadians did per person. The United States had more malls per person. It was retail over-kill. A balancing of the market was inevitable and that balance is what caused the current, modern-day retail apocalypse that is discussed in this book.

We are taught and shaped to buy when there is a sale. It is all about the sale and everybody holds sales. Even when we have one of whatever that is on sale, we buy it because the deals are so good at the sales. Sales are a kind of conditioning; humanity loves deals. So what happens when we buy even when we don't need something just because it is on sale? Well that is the beginning of over-consuming or over-purchasing which leads to issues of hoarding. Sales are also related to items, the malls and money. So, those retail power words should also be read to awaken ourselves to what retailing was actually doing to people.

Bobby Dazzler was a very long-term, independent retailer in one of British Columbia's major malls -"M" Mall. It was considered a mom-and-pop operation. Bobby Dazzler did have stores on the street and other malls but "M" Mall was the original store from 1990. From that store, others came along and went when the leases finished or sometimes closed due to them not being profitable. Sales are what retail is all about. If we didn't have sales we would obviously not have been around to enjoy the success of being in the retail game for such a long time. So yes, sales is vital to all businesses as they generate profit and a means to exist. Sales mean money with ability to earn a great livelihood and grow or expand. Sales are contagious since more sales makes retailers just want even more sales. Sales happen due to a number of factors and they are discussed below.

Sometimes people bought just because the staff member really appealed to them. This was especially the case with our "hot" staff. Yes, packaging does matter when it comes to sales. It also helps to have products that cost $5 and go to be sold for $20, $25 or even $40 each. Retail mark-up is crazy and can get thousands of percentages in profit if the item is properly marketed which is exactly what we did. The Bobby Dazzler mark-up was insane. Everybody would sell t-shirts for $20 but Bobby could get $29 for the same shirt. Why? Because we appealed to the senses and had the right staff to generate sales. That is a winning combo. The store had cool products, hot staff and the right beats of music felt as if you were in a continuous rave/trance party on a beach in Ibiza.

Bobby Dazzler was hot but was still a seasonally-based retailer that was in the red till September. From October to December, the windfall of cash was incredible. It was hard to believe that with effort and persistence, a small 1270 square foot store was able to make $20,000.00 a day in sales. Who needed the lotto? The lotto was right here at Bobby Dazzler. It was sometimes surreal, knowing that when you have the right items or stuff to sell, anything is possible. The sales reached really high days in many of the retail malls where all the traffic was. Even the smaller stores that were only 604 square feet made $80,000.00 to $100,000.00 per month. It was unbelievable that the Bobby Dazzler concept worked out so well for sales. We had the jams pumped so high that the next-door neighbors would often come to let us know that we should turn our music down. But, why? When you are having this much fun making money from the sales, who needs to sleep! There was no need to go on vacation either just as was mentioned earlier. Why would anybody want to take vacation from making money, right?! *Party on at Bobby Dazzler* was the girls' motto. The sales of the store were significant for a small, independent retailer.

We could net $150,000.00 - $250,000.00 per location. So, sales were great and so was the profit for an independent.

Sales gives one drive and momentum of achievement. It is fun! So lets face it, not everyone is able to sell. The best salespeople need to be sought. The staff make the store or break it. Every individual is different but Bobby Dazzler did have some zodiac signs that outsold others by a long shot. Maybe it was coincidence or just weird luck but it still happened. So some of the best signs for retail sales over the years were Sagittarius, Libra and Aries. These three signs seemed to dominate the staff selection over the years. Going through the entire 125 or more staff, it was discovered that the successful staff at Bobby Dazzler fell into these signs more than 50% of the time.

Bobby Dazzler also found that the ideal time to hire our sales staff was when the prospective employee was a youth. The 14-year-old to the 19-year-old had the most to offer. They had incredible drive, motivation, energy and they also seemed to be the ones that stayed the longest when we started out in retail. During the early years, the best were extremely motivated, always had something to prove and wanted to work extra hard to earn money. This was seen right from 1990 to 2017. Youth were the ones that could work the best in our store since they were also the consumers of our products. There were exceptions of course, as time went on. The energy, enthusiasm and drive seemed to dwindle significantly with the advent of social media, cell phones, ipads and computers. Some youth attempted to play the entitlement card or just wanted to spend time texting friends rather than on sales. This had to be addressed as time went on and the abuse of social media seemed to hinder their duties, expectations and tasks. Over the years, social media was actually quite frustrating from a bricks and mortar point of view. But there were mostly great salespeople out there. Some of the staff were so good at sales that they were able to sell a bear out of their skin. So in order to make the sales, the staff had to be the best.

Bobby Dazzler was known as a top seller. This is one of our famous descriptions of selling. Sales gives one that simple high for a few minutes. It is rewarding if one loves to sell and be helpful. You've "got what's hot" then sales are that much easier. Bobby Dazzler was there for the sales so we found certain aspects in the approach taken for sales to be significant when the salesperson approached clients.

The following are some successful techniques for strong sales:

- Essential to be very enthusiastic, slightly forceful and a little aggressive especially when selling items that nobody needed.
- Making a product appear as if a client actually needs it when it is really just a want is the aim of sales.
- Staff really needed to believe in the stuff that a store sells. Nobody can make sales if they don't like the items. It is important the staff love the items and believe in them 110%.
- Sales are only possible if the staff have product knowledge. It is crucial for staff to read the instruction booklet on the item so it can properly explained when it is being sold to a potential client.
- Staff must be able to close the sale professionally. Closing is like putting the item into the bag before it is even sold. Once, the item is handed to the client to examine then it is 50% sold if the staff is able to convince the client that it is already theirs.
- Staff needed to be really comfortable with the items. Since our store sold novelty items that included some party paraphernalia that was sex-oriented, the staff needed to be really comfortable with the clients and treat them like friends.
- Sales cannot happen in a messy store. Sales happen in a clean and organized environment. The store must be spotless!
- Sales happen when a team has a Manager that leads the sales team. One person must be able to lead the part/full-time staff. They need to have all the organizational skills that are necessary for the proper day to day operations of a retail store.
- Consistency in the retail experience is absolutely necessary. All clients must enjoy the same experience as the last client. No playing favorites even if staff are tempted; some clients are more fun than others, for sure.
- The store must be neat, clean and looking the same for all clients.
- One of the most fantastic sales features is when products are sold in a way that the buyer hardly realizes he or she has been sold to. The staff are just old friends of all the clients which makes it easy to sell to them.
- Being too honest about an item can hurt sales even if the product is not all that great. Sales for products that need to be cleared out should be reduced in price and blown out rather than being pumped up as being great products, as those products will just come back on returns or exchanges which is a hassle.

Money

Having a retail book without talking about the great wealth that can be made in the retail world is a book that is incomplete. All people go into business to make money. Bobby Dazzler went into retail to make money. Money is related to sales. Sales equals money which is profit. So, on a positive note, a lot of money can be made in retail, especially if the concept is a winning one. By 1996, it was normal to make 20K in one day at the "M" Mall location during the high season. This is just one store. There were other locations so it literally rained money. Margins were extremely high. Lava lamps that were 18.5 inches back in the day went for between $100.00 to $125.00. Those same lamps are $24.99 online today. So things changed with the advent of more retailers and with the online businesses expanding later. Plus, a retailer like ours could always rely on Halloween, Christmas and other seasons to come every single year which would bring sales and money.

In 1996, the economy was great for our type of store. There was no need to go home because the money was so good. The last Friday before Christmas Day was always a guaranteed lotto. It appeared that if the right products were found, brought in the store to sell and like magic there would be money. A lot of money. So going into retail was very lucrative and not as negative as it appears in the rest of the book. Without sales there are no profits and without profits, there is no money to make a livelihood. Bobby Dazzler would never have stayed in the retail business if it wasn't profitable. However, from inception in 1990 to the closing down of the store in 2017, profitability and money had changed. Challenges, issues and learning occurred that needed to be shared about retail. Like many businesses, retail is subject to many cycles. There are ups and downs in business which means sometimes the money is great and sometimes it is not.

After the economic crisis of 2008, the retail industry never really seemed to be the same when it came to clients' spending habits, credit, debts and having extra money. A shift had taken place in the way people spent money and this drastically changed retail. This was accelerated by the many other different factors that started to impact retail. These factors all affected sales so the money was not as good as it used to be in the good old days. Some of those factors include heavy debt loads and mortgage foreclosures galore that required banks to be bailed out and extreme pressure on the economy that left many jobless. These factors all combined to create a retail environment that was never going to be the same. Examining retail is crucial, since it is the consumer level of spending that takes place right at the heart of the general population. Retail speaks volumes about the amount of confidence the general public has to actually spend. That confidence in being able to spend money had definitely been depleted by 2008.

RENOS

Renos is short for renovations. Part of the retail business is the renovation of a space to suit the needs of the retailer. Retailers must take a unit in the condition that has been agreed upon by the landlord and the tenant to the final state of being a fully operational retail store. The retailer is required to update the space to suit the needs of the store that they wish to put in. This generally requires an extensive number of renovations. Renos cost a lot of money. Bobby Dazzler had gone through a total of seven store renos from 1990 to 2017. These renovations were from the shell space to a fully operating store that required electrical, drywalling, plumbing, sprinkler heads, flooring, slate wall, decorative neon lighting, shelving, tiling and all the building permits required for such work. The entire process is referred to as adding leasehold improvements to the unit. There are significant costs associated with this process, along with time. Typical store renovations for Bobby Dazzler cost anywhere from as little as $75K to $150K depending on the size of the store that Bobby Dazzler took. Costs for other retail businesses obviously vary and can be cheaper or much greater depending on the size of the location and the type of work that is required to update the space to fit the needs of the retailer. This money obviously needs to be expensed out properly so that store renos come within budget.

Having a background in general trades, general contracting and construction is an absolutely necessary skill that is handy when dealing with the various trades, even if a general contractor is going to be hired, so that prices are not highly inflated. Otherwise, the retailer is subjecting themselves to be ripped off with the tender offers that come in. Sure, getting really experienced and reputable companies might be the right way to go but often they were the ones that were most overpriced. Bobby Dazzler generally used the services of the smaller, independent contractors and took on the duties of being the general contractor ourselves. Without getting into the specific how-to's, do's and don'ts of renos, specific retail stores require certain construction requirements. If a project, tradesperson or contractor is giving outrageous prices like anything in life, it is best to get a second, third or fourth or more opinion of what to do. It should be pointed out that a trusted General Contactor is usually the best route when a retailer has NO construction experience. This avoids problems, issues and going over-budget or the possibility of not being able to open on time as per the lease agreement. Renos in the retail world are always very expensive projects so it is wise to seek advice from those that have experience in the trades, tendering of projects and general contract works. It should be noted that if a store does NOT complete the renos on time due to delays, the onus is on the retailer to pay heavy-duty fines per day to get the store open. Those fines can be steep. Some of our leases had fines that were as high as $2,500.00 per day if the store is not opened upon the lapse of the fixturing period. The fixturing period is a period of time allotted to the retailer to do the renos to a space to make the space useful to the needs of the store.

Being a woman was really challenging in the retail world. But the real challenge came when trades came to provide a tender offer for a job. Nobody would take Bobby Dazzler seriously. Most trades even asked to speak to my husband, dad or brother. Yes, right here in Canada. Wow! This just resulted in many, many tender offers having to be made before an offer could be accepted and moved on. Contractors did not treat women the same way when a job needed to be done. Over time, this was seen over and over again. An example was the first electrical tender for the first store that was built. The offer came in at $40,000.00 for a 1640 square-foot store. A total of 12 offers were taken into consideration, all from reputable firms. The final offer that was eventually acceptable was for $10,750.00 plus taxes. Sure, they had some extra stuff/additions added to the bill but it wasn't more than $1,275.00 according to the final invoice. There is a really big difference with the high bid of $40k to the final price of approximately $12K. It was just mind boggling how each and every contractor worked in the exact same manner. Contractors would come in, give ridiculous tenders that were clearly overpriced. There were so many instances that Bobby Dazzler was made to feel incompetent by contractors that it was sad to see. There was no reason that was going on other than the fact that a woman wanted to get a fair price for the work being tendered on.

Renos are part of the retail world and they can be frustrating since leases require the retail store open for business on a certain date. In some instances, leasehold improvements can be undertaken by the landlord who already has a set of contractors that they already work with. This can be ideal as all work is left up to the landlord. It may even be advantageous for a small retailer that has NO experience in dealing with construction, trades or renos. However, this particular scenario was never an option for Bobby Dazzler. Normally, landlords gave Bobby Dazzler 60 days to improve the space for our use. We would try to complete the project as fast as possible in order to open for business early to take advantage of some free rent days which we put into our lease agreement/proposals. Bobby Dazzler eventually got efficient enough that by 2007, we were able to do an entire store renovation from shell space to retail store in 30 days. This required coordination, proper planning and of course connections to the right people. Using the same group of trades helped as they had proven themselves and provided the right price for the work that was asked of them within the time frame needed without any non sense. Many contactors that were accepted actually liked the idea of being able to work nights as they had other jobs in the daytime so this extra work for our small retail store was just extra money for them. However, larger contractors didn't like to work at night which was sometimes required since the landlord was very, very fussy about the amount of noise that took place which interfered with the quiet enjoyment of the other tenants. So larger contractors were actually more expensive during the night as they charged double time for night work. This is where using the small contractors made sense. They didn't charge extra or double the money to work after hours due to noise restrictions.

Some large and medium-sized landlords also provided tenants with incentives by offering leasehold improvement allowances. These leasehold improvement allowances were per square foot for renovation purposes in order to assist a long-term tenant off-set the expenses of renovations. Bobby Dazzler was lucky enough to get allowances for all the leases that it signed, especially for the leases that were five years or ten years in length. This allowance could be free rent for two to six months or a flat rate amount per square foot, usually around $25-$50 if we were lucky. It all depended on the landlord and how deep their pockets were. But it is important to know that landlords can give some allowances and these should be negotiated into the lease at the time of lease dealings.

Novel

Bobby Dazzler's wares were novel. The store was a novelty retailer of gifts, gadgets and novelties associated with party wares, seasonal products, drinking and smoking products. Being a novelty retailer means that something that was fun and exciting one day, may not be so fun the next. Bobby Dazzler could not take returns back to the store. Thus, we had to strictly enforce a policy of *NO REFUNDS but Store Credit* policy. Store credit means a credit is still remaining in the store for goods that can be purchased at a later date for the amount of the goods that was returned. We did allow for exchanges on unopened, non-seasonal products that could be re-sold. We also allowed for customers to exchange a product within 10 days of purchase if the item did not operate or was defective. So it was not a strict policy that nothing was coming back but we had some allowances for exchanges.

Many retailers are learning that return policies need to be updated. Large business is easily able to take returns in a generous manner. However, smaller retailers are really impacted by client returns so an independent retailer cannot just take an item back for NO reason. It could never survive! Large department stores can allow for returns in 14 days, 30 days, 45 days, 60 days and in some cases 90 days. Well, this is due to them being "large" department stores. Bobby Dazzler did notice that many retailers started to adopt the no-refund policy even in the fashion industry. Stores no longer provided a refund but a store credit so that the value of the refunded item could be used at the store at a later time without having the give the cash or credit back to the client. This business model was put into play by many of the mid-level and large fashion retailers. They, too, found that even fashion can be novel one day and found to be blasé the next

FLOOD

This topic seems a little weird to talk about when it comes to retail. However, disasters happen in retail! Bobby Dazzler had to deal with many types of disasters. Disasters such as fires, vermin, vandalism, theft and floods can all happen in retail. All problems must be reported to the landlord or security immediately. That is indicated in the lease. Minor problems like rats and vermin must be dealt with by the individual tenant unless the vermin was coming from the food court. Food court tenants are often plagued with this problem but it usually gets taken care of pretty quickly, especially if the landlord wants to have clients come to eat at the mall in the future. That is when the landlord gets involved big time as it was obviously bad for the food court business and the mall's reputation if vermin was present in the complex.

Dealing with any of above major or minor disasters requires the retail to be adequately insured, for sure. All landlords required retailers to carry proper insurance and have to produce an insurance certificate prior to being able to operate a retail business in their complexes, malls, and strip malls. In fact, the Certificate of Insurance is a document that needs to be provided to the landlord every single year as part of a clause in the lease. Insurance covers many of the disasters that happened in retail but minor problems of theft cannot all be covered since the deductible is so high. When insurance didn't cover it, the landlord was actually very helpful in compelling a neighboring tenant to pay up for problems that were caused by their negligence. This was the case in half of the minor floods since they fell below the $1,500.00 deductible. Bobby Dazzler still got paid by the responsible neighbor due to another clause in the lease that actually allows the landlord to pressure the tenant responsible for the damage to pay for losses incurred by a tenant due to their negligence by leaving a sink running all night, flushing grease or oil down a toilet, and other smaller issues that cause a minor disaster, but still a disaster, nevertheless.

In our retail store, Bobby Dazzler went through a total of six floods that resulted in a number of insurance claims needing to be filed for each and every single one of them. We were located underneath the food court and under the food court washrooms so this might be the reason we had so many floods. Each flood resulted in a loss from as little as $1,000.00 to as large as $50,000.00. The smaller claims were either paid out by the landlord or by the neighboring tenant who was found to cause the problem and was liable. Our deductible was $1,500.00. Floods are common not just because of the food court but water from rain, leaky roofs and weather causing major disasters in malls. Retailing in the mall also means that space is being shared with other tenants. These other tenants forget to shut off the water like our neighboring dentist did at "M" Mall and let the water run until security called at 2 am to let us know that our store was totally flooded. After getting there, it appeared that nothing could be done about the loss of product except to look on the bright side that new products could be ordered to replace the wet, stale inventory that was water damaged. By examining the larger flood that took place in the middle of the night, the retailer needs to be aware that just because insurance is in place, it doesn't mean that the payout is going to take place fast.

Sometime in 1997, a restaurant behind Bobby Dazzler started to dump grease down their toilet. Yes, their toilet, and not dump it properly in a grease trap that was provided for them by the mall. Well, guess what happened? A major, massive flood that brought about 8-10 inches of water into Bobby Dazzler overnight. Ouch! After getting inside the store with rain boots, we could see that a lot of the inventory in the stockroom was destroyed since it was on the floor. Delicate products were kept on the shelves so glassware was okay. Security took pictures of the whole thing for the mall. We called our insurance company who showed up first thing in the morning to assess the damage, make a claim and take more pictures. It looked like the store was going to have close for about two or three weeks. The carpets were all soaked and the store smelled like sewage with grease and oil due to it being a toilet backed up. We would need to order new inventory, get paid for profits lost during that two-week period and get new carpet put in or have it dried by dryers. This was not the worst of it either. The insurance company would drag their feet when it came time to pay. The insurance company needed to go over the books for the last two years so that an average could be established for the two or three weeks that the store was going to be closed. So they hired an outside accountant to do it. We needed to drop off the last two years of records to their office. We did this fast and it sounded simple. Yet, the accountant took his time going through all the records to get an average per day loss for those two weeks. We needed to pay rent from our own pockets even though the store was closed. The rent would be reimbursed but that wasn't going to be fast. We needed to order inventory to replace what was lost out of our own pockets as insurance claims take time to pay out. Dealing with insurance companies was a draining experience. No pun intended.

Some money was advanced within a month, but the final claim for the damages was now hovering over $50,000.00, and it would only be paid once the insurance company did a credit check on Bobby Dazzler to see if we had good credit. We couldn't believe that is what the fine print in our insurance policy required. Our policy was paid and our store never had any major claims except for this one. Everything was fine but it should be pointed out that the final payment came about 15 months after the flood. One's credit could get screwed if payments are not being made for inventory, rent and expenses while the claim is being examined during that 15-month period. Or the business may cease to exist if it is already not doing well, if a longer period of loss took place due to a fire which would take longer for a payout to take place. What would have happened if the credit report came back with a poor score? Does that mean that the insurance company would not have to pay us out? Would this have meant that our business would simply go bankrupt due to this flood despite being up to date on our insurance? These are things that the retailer needs to know and be aware of.

We learned as we went through this disaster but a retailer must have ample financial backing for those rainy days, flood days that happen in the retail world. Generally speaking, dealings with insurance companies can be tricky, lengthy and possibly financially draining. On the plus side of this rather expensive insurance claim, we got rid of a lot of old inventory and ordered new inventory that sold faster. The owner and all the staff got two and half weeks off away from the store to have a mini staycation at home but there was still stress/worry over the loss that took a long time to pay out? At the end of the day, the whole point of discussing this flood is essentially to draw attention the fact that insurance companies are difficult to deal with when it comes to major losses/disasters. A retailer should be prepared financially to deal with the unforeseen circumstances that arise.

A couple of other disasters that can take place which many people don't even think about are the power going out in the mall. Major power outages in the mall are a huge problem especially when the four that Bobby Dazzler experienced happened during the busy retail season of Christmas. The landlord is supposed to have back-up generators in order to ensure that the mall can remain open if a power failure occurs. Unfortunately, the times that Bobby Dazzler experienced power outages, the generators did NOT kick in. The store had to close early despite there being huge line ups with clients who were willing to make huge purchases. This is extremely frustrating and it is a disaster that the insurance company will not honor nor will the mall, as there is typically, a clause that absolves the mall from any responsibility for losses due to an act of God or weather problems.

The next problem which may seem small but is actually a major problem is the credit card processing machine going down. Often the machines can break down. These machines operate not just with electricity but also use the telephone line or internet connection in order to dial up a connection with the host computer in order to generate an approval code for all credit and debit card transactions. If the internet connection is down, the machine cannot get an approval code. It may be best to get a wireless system that doesn't deal with either a telephone line or an internet connection that is plugged in. This problem seemed to happen once per year and it always happened in December during the busy Christmas season. The best way to deal with this problem is pay the credit card processing company extra money to have a replacement terminal sent within four hours as that is an optional service that major credit card processors provide if a retailer is willing to pay for the extra service. In the meantime, credit card transactions are processed manually with the use of the old school imprinter and by obtaining verbal/oral authorizations from Mastercard, Visa or American Express. These transactions are entered into the debit terminal once it is operational again.

Books

The importance of keeping organized books and records was not just taught in high school in Accounting and Business but it was also seen when a job at CRA (Canada Revenue Agency) was landed in 1987 and 1988 during the Grade 11 and Grade 12 years. Bobby Dazzler learned a lot about keeping good records from CRA. CRA is the Canadian tax department while the United States deals with the IRS (Internal Revenue Services). Other countries in Europe and Australia would have different names for their tax departments. Since CRA was located one block from my high school, they looked for top performers to work during their tax season in the mail room as T1 General processors. Learning to keep accurate books and records right at the tax department at the age of 16 and 17 taught me the importance of carrying on this skill into retail. To start a successful retail business, for that matter any business, keeping books and records in order is essential. CRA had a policy that any document that arrived in their office including the envelope must be stapled. If other "stuff" arrived with the T1 general, that too must be kept since some people actually paid in change/cash or with postage stamps. It was one of the best learning experiences that one could have and it paid really well too.

It was a job that really resonated with what Bobby Dazzler was doing in high school. Spending extra time at lunch learning Accounting and Advanced Accounting also resulted in my being the top Business Education student in Grade 12 among 1500 students. I knew that business was it. Going through books was also handy when looking for new and exciting products to sell. Books, as in catalogs, are an essential part of the business when searching for unique and innovative stuff to sell in the store. Books are a part of the retail world just as much as they are part of the business world.

It should be pointed out that the tax department is not the only one that may be interested in the books of a retailer. Accurate books must be kept for the landlord as the landlord does have a clause in the lease that enables them to perform an audit on the books and records of the retail business. Retailers often pay percentage rents to the landlord for sales that go over and above a certain threshold. Sometimes a retailer may under-report sales, and that would be discovered in a landlord audit. Bobby Dazzler experienced two such audits in our 27 years of operating our business. Both audits took place at our main, high-performing store at "M" Mall. Our books and records were perfectly clean in both instances.

Books and records must also be kept for insurance companies when a claim is filed. As mentioned earlier when discussing certain disasters like a flood, an insurance company often hires an external accountant to audit the books in order to obtain an average for the losses that may occur. External accountants have the same standards as CRA and landlord accountants when auditing a business for an insurance claim payment.

These are just some of the reasons accurate books and records are necessary for a retail business. Each country has different governmental agencies and agencies that may require an audit. That can researched by an individual business prior to going into to a retail business. Nevertheless, the books and records of a business must be organized and in order at all times.

Right

The customer is always "right": that is the way customer service has been viewed in the retail world for a long time. Especially with big-box or large retailers who are able to exchange or return products long after the 30, 60, 90 or 120 days exchange/return periods have lapsed. Smaller retail stores like Bobby Dazzler could not possibly survive based on this lenient policy of the "customer is always right" just to retain future business. It just wouldn't be profitable or make any business sense.

However, there were so, so many clients who felt that they were RIGHT when they would come back and realize that we do not do REFUNDS that some very interesting stories arose. Some of the stories include:

1. Throwing the product at the sales clerk on many occasions.

2. Screaming, yelling and throwing a temper tantrum inside the store like a little toddler. Yes, security was called to have them removed.

3. Bringing in the Bible and stating that they did not try on the edible underwear and the missing candy off the G-string candy underwear came like that from the package.

4. Claiming the brown marks and stains on the t-shirt came on the shirt when purchased yet they didn't notice them when they picked up the shirt at time of sale nor did the sales clerk who would have clearly seen 10 inch black stains on the t-shirt. Ewwh!

5. Claiming the store sold a totally smashed up lava lamp leaking oil/wax from the box and can't even be picked up out of the bag due to extensive damage that had occurred after being dropped while it was being transported home.

6 Returning superhero underwear with stain that was there the whole time. Eeehw! Nobody wants to touch that!

7. Telling the sales clerk that our store sold two broken drinking glasses that were just wrapped up in bubble wrap five minutes prior to them leaving the store. Until we mention that we heard their bag drop outside the store and the "bang!" I mean, really?....this is not McDonald's where you get a new Big Mac after dropping it.

8. Clients saying they need their $10 back because rent is due today. Really?!?

9. An adult saying that they need their money back because their boyfriend would break up with them if they don't get their $20 back NOW.

10. Clients stating that they would call their daddy or big friend if we didn't refund their money, then, threatening that they would be waiting for the clerk at their car after work.

11. Clients threatening to call security or police if we didn't refund the $25 product.

12. Clients threatened to call CRA (Canada Revenue Agency) if we didn't give them their money back.

13. Clients refusing to leave the store. An actual sit-in at the store for 2-3 hours as a means of protest, and eventually just walking out.

14. Demanding to speak to the owner of the store because they failed to see the 2 foot by 4 foot sign in black and white that read, "NO REFUNDS AND EXCHANGES WITHIN 7 DAYS" - exceptions apply to the exchange policy. Plus, the same was written on their receipt.

15. Claiming that they would post negative comments in the newspaper about our store policy. This did happen, yet the following Monday was an incredibly busy day in sales given all the negativity that was printed in the local newspaper.

16. Threatening to take to Facebook, Twitter and/or Instagram so that our business would go bankrupt because we didn't refund their $20 item. Do people actually have time to do this? Yes, they do! That is why we had a policy of NO Bobby Dazzler Facebook, Twitter and Instagram. People love voicing the bad experience which they hope will hurt business. If a business has been around 27 years then it couldn't have been that bad!

17. I need my money because I won't come here again ever. Well, it appears that this client made it in once but we recognize them as a regular.

18. I don't like this ugly Christmas sweater as it wasn't ugly enough purchased on November 23 and would like to have a refund on January 13. Like really, how many wears and parties has this sweater been through and now the client wants their money back or an exchange two months later for a seasonal item. Like, really!?! This happened a lot! Actually, a Christmas sweater could not be returned the next day as it could have been worn that night to an ugly Christmas party. Not even on an exchange.

19 Telling a clerk that they need party lighting products for a birthday party for the night. Coming back the next day and telling the same clerk that they didn't work out the way were supposed to so "I demand all my money back, NOW!" Sorry, no can do! We don't even make any rental money for these items. Using products for one night at a business's expense is not good for our business.

20. Asking if it is possible to do a return of an item purchased a year and half ago. Sure there were exceptions like once or twice a year when it was just clear that we should give a refund because we didn't have a similar product to exchange it for. But, generally, the customer could not always be RIGHT for a small retailer to stay in business and actually be profitable. Otherwise, there was too much room for abuse and unfairness.

21. Is this credit note still good from 1995? Sure, if somebody can keep a piece of paper for 23 years, we can take that, for sure!

At the end of the day, a business needs to have a refund and exchange policy that makes business sense. No business can survive with a policy that is so liberal that customers will abuse the policy. Dollar stores have a NO REFUND AND NO EXCHANGE POLICY. Simple as that! Recently, even large fashion stores are adopting policies of NO CASH/CREDIT REFUNDS but an in-store credit or gift card policy which enables the retail business to retain the profits and just provide the clients an opportunity to get different items. This is the best method by far for any small, medium or large store. Retail stores are in it for the profit. Profit must be retained with policies that actually help the stores remain in business. Otherwise, the retail apocalypse only gains more momentum with liberal policies that cause stores to close their doors for good due to refund and exchange abuse.

STAFF

Bobby Dazzler was a mom and pop operation in the beginning so it was easy to control staff as family was hired. Family did perform well, paid attention and never stole from the business so from that perspective, hiring family as staff can be beneficial. Family has a vested interest in seeing the retail store succeed. Family didn't make outrageous demands and were reliable. Family only left when they got married or went to a job that they studied for. They never just got up and left or called/texted saying that they aren't coming in due to some frivolous reason. Family knew that Bobby Dazzler had expectations and those expectations were to show up, open the store and sell. Family took the business seriously and it was easy to give bonuses to family because they were family. However, after the additional locations began to open up it become necessary to hire staff from the outside. That is when the real challenges were learned of just how difficult it was to get retail staff.

The retail world is notoriously famous for having one the highest turnover rates for staff when compared with other industries. Why is staff such an issue in retail when staff is one of the key elements to any successful business? Just not retail! Some issues that Bobby Dazzler had with staff were common problems that many other retailers faced. Just to list a few, they were the following:

1. Retail jobs are found to be boring and repetitive. This boring, repetitive type of task makes it hard for young people to stay motivated unless there is an incentive for them. Bobby Dazzler made task lists for staff so that they had duties and tasks to fulfill during their shift. This prevented boredom and provided retail staff a sense of purpose.

2. There is little training and the pay is usually very low plus there might be no benefits. However, Bobby Dazzler was able to retain staff by providing commission, daily/monthly or seasonal bonuses based on performance. Bobby Dazzler also offered employee benefits after one year of working so that staff was kept in place. The store also provided staff a 50% discount off all products so the staff could purchase our items inexpensively.

3. There is little chance for advancement, so doing a great job may be seen as futile if an employee is not self-motivated. Staff was kept motivated by providing an ideal work environment along with commissions, bonuses and staff discounts for products. Advancement

was definitely provided to staff once it was determined that they showed initiative. Assistant Store Manager positions and Store Manager positions were available after six months once staff members had proven themselves with no tardiness, no absenteeism and great sales along with a good work ethic.

4. Hiring young people today to the work force also meant that some came with entitlement issues that were related to their ego or improper parenting whereby it was difficult to train staff that didn't want to listen or weren't really interested in learning since they knew everything already. This problem was much more evident with the advancement of social media and the popularity of cell phones.

5. Some employees didn't take retail as seriously as they should since it was normally their first job. So, employees just slacked off or quit or were fired within three months. This non-serious nature of young staff was countered by offering staff discounts and incentives like bonuses so staff would stick around. It also became apparent that open communication was necessary.

6. Unfortunately, employees leave quickly after three-six months once another retail job comes along that pays a little better or offers better discounts at the place of work. Thus, green pastures elsewhere lured some staff away. Retail staff seemed to get bored easily so staff would just change for the sake of change. Staff expected promotions quickly and asked for rewards often. This maybe due to the fact that their experience in high school was based on progressing through school, sports and extra curricular activities where rewards quickly for good performance.

7. If an employee is in school, some of them find that it is too difficult to manage both a job and school, thus they are not able to multi-task or balance two priorities in life at the same time along with their social time. So they decide to focus on school, after only 3 months of working. At the time of hiring, we would ask that the potential employees bring in their report card/transcript of grades along with attendance/tardiness records from high school. Despite being a student with NO work experience, a report card/transcript did show their school performance. There was a strong correlation between good grades and being a good employee. Naturally, students who attended school were more likely to come to their job with little tardiness and were much more serious in their approach to work at

the store. This was always a great idea to ask for at the interview. The store was successful in finding great employees based on report cards and attendance records. Locating staff by requesting transcripts was a fantastic way to find potential, long-term staff.

8. Some employees came in and said they had to quit because their mom or dad told them to. This happened to stellar students with great grades. Parents never liked it when their grades slipped while they were in school. Bobby Dazzler found that B students were best for retail as they seemed to manage keeping their grades while being able to juggle work. Hence, maintaining a balance was important in staff: not to give students so many hours that they would not be able to handle school and work. Bobby Dazzler found that 8-15 hours per weeks worked best for students.

9. Employees found the retail world too complicated, all of a sudden when thrown into a job without proper training. Having to deal with so many people face to face was an issue for some of the employees/ teens who were so used to dealing people through a screen. This was more of a problem going onwards from 2007.

10. Leaving the retail industry to pursue work in another industry that has shorter hours or more flexible hours was another problem but this normally didn't happen until an employee finished college or university. Leaving retail to pursue a job a young adult studied for in school made more sense. So, inevitably staff that went to school would have to leave.

11. Staff also leave quickly due to lack of experience when seeing others who perform better than them. Thus, shying away from the retail job because it involves too much interaction with clients or actual "work". As time went on, Bobby Dazzler found that many teens were just not qualified to deal with the public but better able to deal with people through a phone or screen. This was odd but it did happen.

12. The best way to recruit staff was by word of mouth. Retail staff that was leaving other retail stores after working for many, many years due to their own store closing or moving out of the mall made for great staff being readily available. Malls also had a website that showed who was hiring, so posting on the mall website was definitely a great place to start.

13. Some of the best sales staff had common characteristics that Bobby Dazzler noticed over the years. Those characteristics were positive attitude, great grooming, being proficient in the English

language, a love for the store and products sold at Bobby Dazzler and being self-motivated. Staff found in newspapers were never the best from our experience. Potential staff that came in who applied to the Manager/Owner in a ready to be interviewed manner were the best. Staff that could actually carry an interview on the spot were really great candidates. It appeared that they just wanted the job, badly.

14. Moving forward, employers should look to staffers without judgment and resentment, and lead rather than try to control them. Staff are a resource and not the problem. Taking an open minded approach to staffing seemed to work the best. Getting young staff's points of view can help the business make money since they are at the front of any retail business.

Over the years, Bobby Dazzler was lucky as we found that employees could be retained for longer periods of time if they were offered higher than minimum wages once they got past probationary periods of 3/6/9 months or one year. Employees who were committed were given 1% commission on net sales made by them after one year. This kept staff in place for years. Sharing the profits really paid off. There were also seasonal bonuses when sales went past target and when sales quotas for the month were being reached. Products and items sold in the store were sold to staff at 50% off so there was no need to steal, and theft was never really an issue, especially employee theft. Bobby Dazzler just asked that staff pay us for the cost of the items so we weren't profiting off of our staff either. Sharing the profits and good times with staff made staff very consistent at Bobby Dazzler. Our average long-term staffer stayed four to six years which is significant given the high turnover retailers experience. Sure, there were periods where we too could not find the "right" person. But, once we did, the other sales people just come in and a solid team was built. After running four locations and one kiosk, the magic can be in the staff along with the items that we sold. Here are some recruitment ideas for staff for the retailer:

- Employee referrals are still the best way to get staff. Asking staff who already worked in the store was a great start. People like to work with people they like.
- Bobby Dazzler knew its audience and this was important. Hiring staff who were similar to the clients that we sold to was important. They "get it" and were able to sell it!
- Storefront signs worked great for Bobby Dazzler. We were in

high-traffic malls so the signs were easily visible. Great staff just walked by the store and came in. They were the shoppers of our store.

- The mall had a general website and social media sites that had heavy followings. The followings were greater than our own website. So, advertising on the mall social media site was very productive. Candidates found our posting on the mall's site, Twitter, Facebook and Instagram sites.
- Our customers were also a great source when we looked for staff. They could spread the word quickly. People want to help other people that they had a good experience with.
- Looking towards our neighbor or our competitors was also a good place to go. Bobby Dazzler did poach sometimes when it was necessary. And there are no rules against this practice. Just know that a competitor could poach your staff too.
- Former employees who worked great and could be hired again are also excellent people to get in touch with. This was great for seasonal staff like Christmas or summer. Some ex-employees had summer, winter breaks and still needed employment again. These were great people as there was no training needed again except for the new products that had arrived.
- Searching and having postings at the local high school, college, university or community center was also a great place for Bobby Dazzler. It also got the community involved.
- The last feature that Bobby Dazzler could easily offer to potential employees was a fun and exciting environment. The store played great music, had great products and it was a really fun place to be. It was not boring so by offering a fun environment, Bobby Dazzler differed from the shoe or fashion store next door. It was different! Items fly off the shelves when it is a fun place to work. Giving respect to the staff and treating them in an environment that shares the energy gives staff reasons not to leave, but to stay for a long, long time!

Multi

Everybody wants to expand eventually. However, expansion means more staff, more rents, more inventory and more stress with the possibility of more profits. After running a multi-store operation with a staff of 15-20 during peak periods and paying $40-50K per month in rents and rolling in a lot of dough, sometimes multi might not be it. One can learn that having a multi store operation is not always what it's cut out to be. An examination of the whole picture lets us see if running many stores is the best or if is it just nice to have one successful store.

Bobby Dazzler got to multi store level by 1995. After running "M" for five years, we opened another location in a mall which was later nicked named "Slowheed".

This store was only 600 square foot which was half the space that "M" had but it was a very productive store since it was easy to manage with the small square footage plus the rent was manageable. We signed up for 5 years with the option to renew if desired at the end. It was the perfect size for a second store. It did really well during all the seasonal selling periods. Sales were phenomenal at during December (Christmas)~over $100K for 600 square foot in one month is really great for an independent retailer. After a couple more years of running two stores, the desire to grow came again. This time Bobby Dazzler decided to go downtown into a mature mall that was tourist oriented. The lease was only 3 years and there was an option to renew after 3 years. However, this mall proved to be a mistake. The hours of the store were great, it easy to manage, staffing it was easy, it was not a huge production but the sales were not there. It just didn't have enough traffic. So, in business there are some winners and some losers. This one was a loser! Sales just never took off and it started to suck the life out of the other two stores that were profitable. The lease was difficult to get out of, of course, and that is discussed in the chapter *Lease*.

After approaching the landlord for rental relief, an abatement rental scheme was set up. Sadly, the sales were just not there still and Bobby Dazzler had no choice but to pull the plug on this mall in 2000. At the time, Bobby Dazzler was pregnant with our first child and the stress of losing so much money was not going to work for our family. Bobby Dazzler took off in the middle of the night with our inventory, neon, cabinets and anything else that was not attached. We only had about 8 months left but this store was sucking out the cash like there was no bottom. We needed to fix this loser store somehow and we couldn't see it getting any better. It was bleeding the profits from the other two and this could not go on forever. The landlord was quite upset, obviously, and sued. That particular store was under a different limited company so the landlord could not come after the other 2 limited companies at the other two malls. This is why it is very important to examine all the rules when going into retail. One limited company is NOT under obligation to pay the liabilities of the another limited company even if they trade under the same trade name - Bobby Dazzler. Sure, incorporation costs a little bit more in the beginning but it can be a saving grace if one has a multi-store retail empire that has some winners and loser stores.

Later in the year 2000, Bobby tried the whole kiosk idea but it had to be in a busy area. A high traffic, high volume area with lots of people and more tourists that the last mall was missing. Bobby Dazzler dabbled in a kiosk at YVR (Vancouver International Airport). This sounded like fun and interesting at the same time. The lease was short term, only one year. So, there was NO long term commitment. It was only 12 months, what could possibly go wrong. Right?!? The location was in US departures, the hours were really long 7am-7pm, 7 days a week and ouch! We opened the kiosk in the high season of March when spring break happened. Sales were great in the Spring and Summer. There were many tourists, many people traveling to the United States and people bought a lot of stuff at our kiosk. It was super, crazy business and profits were great. But, when Fall and Winter came, those great sales and profits just slipped away. The profits made earlier in the year just paid for the expenses, rent and staffing during the non-peak periods of September to February when there weren't as many travelers as one would think. The airport is not busy all year round. Once the lease lapsed at YVR, we were out of there for sure. The location was too far, staffing was hard, profitable only 6 months of the year and it was a hit or miss kind of business there. Too hot and cold for us! We got to go.

By early 2002, after trying out YVR, Bobby Dazzler got the itch to use those cabinets, inventory and neon that were kept in storage again. We needed a store in Vancouver and wanted it. This time Bobby Dazzler tried a street location in Kitsilano. This is not the Rodeo Drive of Vancouver but it was a fairly busy street on Vancouver's West Side in a residential neighborhood. It had decent traffic, decent rent and we could control the hours. If we needed to close the store early, we could. This store could be manned by one person. So, we opened up in 2002 and now we were back to 3 locations. The store took a hit right away! The night before opening, our store was broken into and the entire opening inventory was hauled away by thieves. Ouch! That meant that we needed to file an insurance claim as soon as possible. This is not good at all. Thank goodness we had insurance and inventory of what we had in the store so that it could be replaced right away since we had just ordered the inventory. The security system was not in place but it appeared that we were being staked out by some thugs. They successfully brought in a big black van and loaded up overnight. Bobby Dazzler could not believe it. The location of this store was supposed to be in the good part of Vancouver. After two weeks, our insurance paid as we needed to open. This insurance claim was handled much more quickly due to the fact that the store could not open for business without it. We ended up ordering products that were a better fit for our store at the end of the day. We signed up for 3 years with the option to renew for 3 additional years. This store was just a break even store. The traffic really was there but just enough to cover expenses. Some profits during Christmas happened but nothing to write home about. We approached the landlord in 2004 and asked if we could leave or if they had anybody who wanted the store. We also asked for rental abatement. This is discussed in abate in more detail. Lucky for us the next door neighbor wanted to expand their flower shop, so we got out of that lease on good terms.

During 2002, the lease in "Slowheed" mall lapsed and Bobby Dazzler decided not to renew due to Wal-Mart opening in the mall and due to the main competitor of Bobby Dazzler coming into the mall. Sales took a nosedive in upon the arrival of both so a business decision was made to get out of that mall as soon as possible. We took our inventory, cabinets and neon and put those into storage until another suitable location could be found.

In 2004, Bobby Dazzler still felt the need for a much better Vancouver presence since closing the Kitsilano store. This was when an ideal spot opened up on the Rodeo Drive of Vancouver, Robson

Street. It was expensive (@ $7,000 per month) but high foot traffic for 600+ square feet was easy to manage with respect to staff. We took it and opened up in November which would be a great time for retail to open as it is just before Christmas. However, just our luck, retail on Robson is not quite the same as it is in the malls. Robson Street is cold, wet, dark and very undesirable for Christmas shoppers who prefer the enclosed malls. This store started to "suck" the life out of "M" in 2004. It was a very, very expensive mistake to open in November especially when it was discovered in November 2004, the "M" mall was going through a massive, major renovation, redevelopment, in order to join two major malls, "M" and Eaton's Center. This project started on the "exact" same month, same week that the Robson Street store opened.

2004 was the worst year in history of Bobby Dazzler. It was a complete financial disaster. Inventory was ordered for the "M" store as in previous years so payables were sky high. The new Robson Street store was stocked in anticipation of a busy selling season of Christmas. However, the "M" started to cripple in sales. Sales plummeted due to scaffolding, hoarding, ladders, access and exits to the mall being inaccessible. The sales during a normal Christmas for this location would be $150-$175K for November and December. They crumbled to $25K for the two months of November and December 2004. We were in serious financial trouble. Of course, this was voiced to the landlord who reduced the rent to half but this still did not help. Staff was let go, inventory became stale, payables mounted and financial problems mounted not just for the business but on a personal level as well. We were nearing bankruptcy of the Bobby Dazzler business by early 2005 after finishing a dismal Christmas.

Suppliers were called to have terms extended for our payables. Since, we had been around for 14 years already, our suppliers were very supportive. Ronny from Relaxus said, "pay me when you can". Bobby Dazzler thought it might be six months or a year. Ronny never called to ask but he was paid by Christmas 2005. Bobby Dazzler was saved from bankruptcy by its suppliers. However, a personal financial hit still took place because rents could not be made at the Robson Street store and the bailiff was called into the store in September 2004. The store was seized and all the inventory, leasehold improvements and massive investment was gone with a blink of an eye. Running a multi-store operation is not easy for any individual but it was even harder if one wanted to maintain a family life with children. After all, the Bobby Dazzler store came before the hubby and the kids. The financial stress in 2004 also caused many personal problems in the marriage which also broke down in 2004 due to a number of reasons that are discussed in *Marry*. Well, hey at least we tried the multi-store concept. "M" survived as it was the oldest of the all stores. This one made the most profits after all and total realization took place that made Bobby Dazzler think that having one successful retail store was better for the stress level, headache level and the benefit of the children. We decided to run only one store after this point. It was just easier to manager and control.

SCAMS

Over the years, it was unbelievable how many different kinds of scams exist in retail. Credit card fraud, theft and B and E (break and enter), counterfeit currency, fake travelers' checks and bounced checks just to name a few. If retail was a jail then it was the worst jail for the scams that people tried. Learning how humanity behaves is best done when one works in a retail store with the general public. There are so many different types of scams that only a small number of types will be discussed. Bobby Dazzler actually experienced thieves who would phone the store to see if we would be willing to charge a card that they found for an amount so that they would be able to get some cash/money instead of merchandise. Obviously, security would be called once they actually came into the store. As if! It was incredible what some people thought that they could get away with. When a Code 10 appears on the Credit Card terminal, a clerk is supposed to call the Merchant Services number assistance. The thieves knew this and would just bail or run. There is no way a sales clerk is going to go after a credit card thief so that call would simply be a waste of time. Bobby Dazzler also saw mall security not engage with these types of crooks. They were just not worth it for safety reasons. If a credit card was approved then the sale was all okay, as it was Visa/MasterCard/American Express that approved the sale themselves. Our merchandise was gone so all Bobby Dazzler had to do was produce the receipt when the request arrived via mail for the dispute or as a chargeback dispute.

Fake travelers' checks and currency were so common in the 1990's and early 2000's. Fake currency was a daily issue but that changed over time as the bills became harder to counterfeit, especially in Canada. Fake credit cards took off like wildfire also and they looked so very real. The cards would not swipe but the numbers on the top of these cards were legit numbers. The credit card numbers were likely taken from the garbage, another credit card or from a skimming machine that stores and keeps numbers from other establishments where fraudsters work. Fraudsters swipe the card through an actual credit card machine and also through a skimming machine designed to steal credit card information to produce counterfeit credit cards for future use. This also evolved over time when the chip cards were introduced so that fraud could be reduced. Writing checks that bounced was a weekly occurrence until debit cards arrived. Checks were never taken after the arrival of the debit card, which reduced bad debts expenses significantly. Clients changing prices to get the lower price was common for a retailer like ours since we didn't use the scanning system but the old-school system of white stickers that were put on with price guns. The biggest scams that took place though were refund scams and fraud. Here is a list of some of the scams or fraud that took place:

- Wardrobe or renting - making a purchase with the intent to use it for the night or short term and then return the item for a full refund
- Returning stolen merchandise from the store for a full refund or credit.
- Receipt fraud was common, too. Items were purchased from different retailer at a lower price in order to get a refund at a store with the higher, in order to pocket a profit.
- E-receipt fraud which was similar to the above, where an item was returned to the store that was purchased for a lower price online in order to profit when returning it to the store.
- Employee fraud took place when an employee assisted in the return of stolen product for store credit or refund.
- Switch fraud is when a old, broken or defective used item is returned for a working model of the same.
- Price switching was the switching of tags on a lower-priced item to the high-priced item in order to get the higher-priced item for the lower price. This happened in our retail due to it using old-school, white stickers.
- Price Arbitrage was purchasing two similar items but one is cheaper, then returning that cheaper item for the value of the higher-priced one.
- Bricking was the purchase of an electronic item then stripping it of all the useable components to render it unusable and then going back to get a full refund or store credit. Cross-retailer/competitor returns happened when an item that was purchased at another store for a lower price and was attempted to be returned at another for a higher price in order to gain profit.

These scams all added up. According to a quick Google search, scams and fraud cost retailers $50 billion a year in the United States. Retailers in the United States deal with over $260.6 billion in returns in 2015 which naturally affect sales. These are huge numbers and affect the bottom line of all retailers. In fact, numbers such as these are so crushing that they only add to the chaos of the retail apocalypse that is taking place in the United States.

Naturally, to counter such deep financial problems associated with refund fraud and scams, retailers are needing to buckle down on refund policies. "No receipt, No refund or credit" are absolutely necessary in order to save a retailer from such abuse. Bobby Dazzler didn't even take refunds but did provide store credit when a receipt was produced. Sure, our store used discretion, especially if the client was a regular. Yet, there were other classic scams such as the little old lady that comes in to get change for $50 bill and confuses the crap out of the sales clerk and walks out with an extra $20 along with the $50 that she wanted broken. This got to many of us time and time again. Or what about the client who said he gave a $20 bill when it was actually a $10 bill that was given, "right" so we have to believe him. The best way to counter this problem was not to put the bills that the client gave us in the till until the transaction was completed. Then, there is the group of teens who broke into the showcases to take all the lighters or broke into the cupboards and take everything inside while the clerk is busy helping one of their friends (the distracter). There was also the swarming technique were a group of kids that swarm the store to each steal an item each while the clerk is busy making an actual sale. Shoplifting was something that took place at least once per day and sometimes more. Ouch! It is just part of everyday retail. The retail prices took this into consideration, of course. The retail prices had to be kept high in order to balance out some of the theft that took place. For personal security reasons, it was never a good idea to go after the thieves.

Nobody ever knows why retail is called retail jail until personally experiencing all of these scams. It was very much a learning experience dealing with the general public which needs to be shared, for others to realize just how difficult it can be retailing even for a small, independent retailer, never mind the large players that experience scams five-fold.

Retail accepts many forms of payment. Retail takes credit cards, debit cards and gift cards. There were so many types of cards in the industry that sometimes it was hard to tell which ones were real and which were fraudulent. Stolen gift cards were quite big by 2017 as they were not chip-embedded like the credit cards and debit cards. Gift cards loaded by employees that were empty when the client just purchased the gift card from the mall. Or gift cards that were issued when no products were even returned. Clients also tried to call our store and order items for themselves when the card belonged to their parents or someone else. This transaction was obviously not going to take place. Credit card sales done via mail order or the phone could be verified by the credit card company as we did not ship anything unless it was being shipped to the address for the credit cards provided at the time of sale. Needless to say, the number of cards and the amount of fraud that took place was simply incredible.

Crooks would come in and entire racks of inventory would be stolen within a blink of an eye. Yes, it happened to us and other retailers. Or, if we forgot to close the front door before going to the bathroom in the stock room when working by ourselves. It appeared as if people were watching to see when the clerk would take a bathroom break. And an attack on the store was possible. Who would think that in 3-4 minutes $500-$1000.00 of merchandise would be swiped. It happened at Bobby Dazzler and at many other retail stores. Theft, fraud and dealing with the crook is part of the retail job. Again, this makes it more difficult to find staff who are assertive enough to deal with this sort of thing without crying their eyes out as it happened.

Then, Bobby Dazzler had to deal with the staff who were the crooks. Staff would actually take items home when the store manager or owner was not around at the end of the shift. It didn't happen a whole lot but it did happen. Bobby Dazzler never used to check the bags of employees because we trusted our staff but staff actually made off with a significant amount of inventory. Our store did offer 50% off all products in order to counter theft so that staff could just pay us the cost price for an item instead of stealing. So, if theft was not taking place at the store by the thieves who came in to take product without payment or by using fake credit cards, the staff was taking inventory. This is really, really hard to deal with. How was anybody to be trusted anymore? These were people who were in place to run the retail store not steal from it. Why was this happening and how is it normal?

Still other thieves would call the store and talk to a clerk who was not familiar with orders and have them agree to have merchandise/

inventory sent to the store that was NEVER ordered. This was completely bogus. Yes, there are companies out there that just phone up retailers and send out boxes and boxes of debit rolls when they were never ordered. Of course, they billed Bobby Dazzler and wanted payment for $1,000.00+ for an invoice for debit rolls that don't even fit our machine. Or we would receive 1000 pens with our store name pre-printed on them. They were so many scams in the malls that it was crazy

There were others scams that took place which were detailed in the chapter, *Pests*. Scams by the pests were a little more sophisticated.

Waste

There is no doubt that retailers generate a lot of waste. It all starts before the retail store even opens up for business. Retailers normally receive a space that is either a shell space or a space that was a retail store previously. A shell space requires a full renovation with construction that includes building, electrical, plumbing, architectural and many other plans/permits to be taken out. All these cost a lot of money. Even if a store is taken that was previously a store, the new store needs to be updated so that the look of the store being renovated is up to par with what the landlord has agreed to and in line what the new retailer is going to be selling according their brand image. Nevertheless, a renovation is still required which does mean that some gutting is required and waste will undoubtedly be generated through the removal of electrical, drywall, plumbing and other materials so that the new store will have the right layout, look and design to suit the needs of the new store. Only when stores are used as temps do minimal amounts of gutting take place. The amount of waste that is generated when a new store goes in is always excessive and ridiculous.

Upon completion of the store, the retailer is open for business but more waste is generated right when inventory starts to arrive. Boxes and boxes of goods are delivered to the store that need to be unpacked, priced and put on shelves. Once the boxes are unpacked, a significant amount of packaging is left over that needs to be recycled. After that packaging is disposed, the consumer deals with the inner packaging. Most products arrive in packaging of their own that consumers must discard once they open the item up. So there is a huge amount of packaging that goes into bringing the item out for being displayed in the store to actual use. Sadly, the packaging often makes the sale for the useless item. We knew this well, as most of the novelty items came with fancy packaging with instructions on how the item worked and what it could do for the client. All of the packaging would be discarded immediately upon purchase and the item would be taken out to enjoy. The packaging that went into most of the items that we sold and the items that most retailers sold was a total waste to the environment . It was largely Styrofoam, plastic and other products that were normally not easy to recycle.

On top of the packaging was the need for the store to provide a bag to bring the item home. This bag was usually printed with the brand and store logo in order to advertise the store name and brand. This was provided at the point of purchase. Even after asking clients at the point of purchase if they would like a bag or not, the client still requested a bag in 75% of the cases. Sure, Bobby Dazzler encouraged shoppers to just put the item in another large bag they had or encouraged the shoppers to use reusable shopping bags. But that didn't work as often as we liked. Usually, the client liked to show that they had shopped in a particular store, especially if the store was an expensive or high-end retailer. It made for their shopping experience to be a real experience. But it also makes the client feel like they are shopping when they have multiple bags from multiple stores. So the more bags the customer has, the more cool it looks to other people who can see that this customer is doing some heavy-duty shopping. It was a strange phenomenon to see them want multiple bags with each and every single purchase. This all seemed a little crazy and obviously not that environmentally friendly from a retail standpoint. To reduce waste of bags, perhaps encouraging clients to bring their own bags into the store which were reusable and providing them a $1.00 discount off the retail price of item that was purchased may work. Or, charging clients for bags so that they refuse to spend the extra money on a bag. Large retailers have already started to do this, especially grocery stores and drug stores.

What about all that inventory that didn't sell? Even after clearance and blowout sales, some inventory was just dead. Nobody wanted it. Some retailers discarded the inventory that didn't sell rather than donating. This discarding of inventory is very prominent in the fashion industry. Bobby Dazzler always donated items that just didn't sell to the Christmas Bureau, the various school districts that were in need and to many shelters or charities that could use some of the products. Our items were never discarded, ever! Fashion retailers have a hard time donating brand-name clothing to the poor since it is seen devaluing the brand. This is unfortunate as many fashion retailers actually discard unsold merchandise and don't recycle it. This is a true waste when we look at the fact that some clothes could be worn by others. Yet some retail stores had strict policies of discarding all clothing and merchandise that didn't sell. Donating was often seen as devaluing the brand. After all, if the poor could wear the brand without paying for it then the middle class or rich would not buy it. These practices do need to change. Ethical consumerism which is discussed later touches on this topic and it is the way that future of retailing will go. It was good karma so why not.

Some retailers still used paper catalogs and coupons. This was a waste for sure, involving printing costs, paper and time when coupons could be provided online or via text. Reducing the amount that is being printed is essential to the going green movement. Some retailers still felt old school is cool when it comes to advertising. Bobby Dazzler just did sales that required no catalogs or coupons. Sales were on every day with your independent retailer.

Marry

Everything that happened, happened at Bobby Dazzler. It is important to make connections and pay attention to who walks in through the front door of the store. Even retailers marry but finding a hubby at the store was really funny and unexpected. After graduating University in 1996, it may have been time to settle down, not just with the business. Sure, business was the first love but even retailers need love. Parents usually put pressure on their Indian daughters to find a suitable mate or else they will find one for us. This was not something that was high on the priority list. After all, the business is first and a retail business is a lot of work. Who wants to marry when you marry the business? It is so much more fun! Being independent for that long a time means that the business fills a certain void. Hence, being busy takes up the time that might be spent on a marriage. It just wasn't something that felt important when so many people were getting married and divorced.

But that all changed, in 1997, when Moshe, my General Contractor, brought his brother to help from Israel. Moshe said that he was going to bring his younger brother so that the store construction which was already two weeks behind could get a jump-start. Well, that sounded like a great idea! Moshe brought his younger brother, Yoram. Yoram shook my hand and said, " I am going to marry you!" No kidding! Bobby Dazzler said, "I think so, too!" This was love at first sight! No, no, not me....this guy was going to take Bobby Dazzler away from the business for sure. After shaking hands, so much for getting some construction done. Bobby Dazzler took off with Yoram to show him all the hot spots of Vancouver, plus more. Yes, we married and it is hard to balance married life for a retailer.

Retailer hours are long. There is no way a retailer can stay till 9 pm every day and expect the marriage to last. Part-time staff needed to be hired so the shift could finish at 4 pm or 5 pm. The normal seven or eight hour day was required. It was good-bye to the 9:30 am-9 pm days. Working retail also means that we are open seven days a week. This too had to be shortened. A single retailer can easily work seven days a week but a married one has other commitments to a relationship. So the weekends needed to be freed up a bit so that some time could kept for the marriage. Saturday was always a busy day so going in from noon to 5 pm was the best way to deal with Saturday sales and to balance a happy marriage. It should be pointed out that even though a retailer is not at their store, they are always thinking about their store when it is open and even when it is closed. It is a very time-consuming profession, especially if you are a small retailer that is the buyer, accountant, store manager, merchandiser, human resource manager, merchandiser, displayer and all the other jobs that a retailer does in order to run an efficient and profitable retail store. These are all jobs that need to fit into a married life which can be challenging if married to a partner who doesn't understand the job is really, really demanding even if the day is done at the store. There is so much extra work that is required outside of the store that these are all things that a retailer needs to understand before deciding to marry.

CHILD

It is never easy for a woman deciding to marry and then having a child while running a multi-store operation that required a lot of attention. Bobby Dazzler decided to have a child in 2000 after two years of marriage. Nevertheless, after having one child, another came along due to not listening to the old wives' tale that you could NOT get pregnant while nursing. This is totally false by the way! Pregnancy can be viewed as being easier when it requires you to be on your feet all the time. The problems of water retention were definitely reduced due to the fact in retail, we don't sit. We are on our feet and walking around the store all the time. This is good for keeping the body in shape and feeling less bloated. Time does go by really quickly during each pregnancy because there is always someone in the store who needs a greeting or help. The 6-7 hour day goes quickly which made each pregnancy go by quickly. Gaining extra weight isn't as much of a problem because there is no large fridge and access to lots of foods that sometimes makes some women gain extra weight. Packing a nutritious lunch was absolutely necessary and it is a hassle to close the store down to go and lunch in the food court when you're pregnant. Owning your own retail store means you could eat whenever you want. If you get hungry, have a snack when you want.

However, running a retail store with a child is a totally different ball park for Bobby Dazzler. In 2000, a woman in Canada did not qualify for UI benefits. They are now called EI benefits. EI meaning (Employment Income) or UI (Unemployment Income) is paid when a woman goes on maternity leave to take care of her newborn child. In 2000, there was no benefits payable to a business owner since they do not pay into the EI/UI program so the costs of having a child and still having to run the retail store are borne entirely by the business owner. Hubby was not a retailer and was unable to take the role of sales person/manager. He was a contractor not a retailer. He could not nurse as formula was not used either so it was a difficult decision but the baby and later, babies, needed to come to the store. This is especially difficult for a new mom who is nursing. But it is your store so you are allowed to do whatever it takes to make sure the business does well. Hiring a part-timer to work alongside while taking care of the babies in the store meant that nothing was missed. After staying home for about four to six weeks and watching the sales plummet at all the stores, there was no choice but to bring a playpen, stroller and mini-crib into the stockroom. It had to be done this way to survive and thrive in retail. Babies sleep so much that with a baby monitor, the store could be run and keeping the baby at the store was the only option. This worked out! It even worked out when the second child came along. In fact, both children learned to walk by holding themselves up along the cupboards of the cabinets. Yes, both children were brought to the retail store and had independent cribs in the stockroom. Lucky for Bobby Dazzler, there was a bathroom, hot water and mini-fridge for food. There was never a need to leave the store. Both children spent the first one and half years of their lives inside the store until daycare took them. Alas, that meant more personal expenses.

On the plus side, the children learned to be around people. They were not scared of people while walking around and became a part of Bobby Dazzler literally. They never left the store either. It was almost as if they knew that the farthest they could go was to the front glass doors and then they would just turn around with their cute soother in their mouth to come back to their spot at Bobby Dazzler.

PLOT TWISTS
&
PERSONAL CHALLENGES

USUAL

Bobby Dazzler was a retail business as usual till around 2003, this is when some juicy ups and downs started to show up. It would have unusual for the Bobby Dazzler retail business just to be a usual business as even the name means something unusual. Many different characters and events started to take place after 2003 which just made the retail story all the more juicy and interesting. Life works in the same types of cycles and nothing happens without a reason. Bobby Dazzler made some positive connections in business and some negative. The unusual events that took place and the personal challenges that were faced by Bobby Dazzler are our version of events and were considered speculation by lawyers when presented with this manuscript. Hence, the book is a "reveal all" from our point of view and from our memories. Retail business is just a usual business after all and many people are involved in it. So things really began to get shaken up around late 2003 hit. It was just a crazy year and the start of a chain of events that seemed to continue till 2018, even when the physical store had closed in mid-2017. The following chapters will provide details of personal challenges, business challenges and crazy happenings that made retail very difficult for Bobby Dazzler.

After going through the financially challenging renovation redevelopment of "M" Mall and suffering a broken-down marriage, there was no gas left for more things to go wrong. But they did. In February 2004, the step-daughter (Noahm) returned to Israel because she just "didn't fit in" at school, at home and everywhere else she went. This issue became a real problem when her father, my hubby, said, "I can't love you if you can't raise her for me!" Wait a minute, I didn't make this kid, I have two of my own children plus I am not the mother who has custody and had the gall to send her Hebrew-speaking-only daughter to Canada on a one-way ticket to her dad so that she could straighten her out at the expense of our family. While all this drama with Noahm is going on, the "M" Mall business was sinking daily due to the excessive noise, construction and blockage of access to the mall, and the hoarding (dry walled storefronts) that blocked access to the store and visibility which caused sales to plummet. This store was the main breadwinner and it supported our family. It was our livelihood that was on the line. Noahm's problems just added to the chaos our home was experiencing with my two little toddlers. Suppliers began to call for invoices that were now becoming due from November and December. The newly opened Robson Street store was doing awful during the rainy, wet season of winter. A financial nightmare was taking place due to the pressure of the failing retail business and the horrible home life that surrounded the issues of the step-daughter and a marriage going down the toilet fast due to this and financial issues. It should be kept in mind that there were two other small children of mine who were only two and three that were also going through this whole mess of fights and yelling. This really couldn't go on for long. There was no peace in this. Personal savings were being drained by the high rents of Robson and the abated rents at "M" Mall. They were still astronomical compared to where to sales had fallen down to. By June 2004, it became unbearable for hubby so he left the house with his clothes in a big black plastic bag. There was no way that I was going to call him back. This was done! All the financial responsibilities for the store and children fell on Bobby Dazzler. Hubby did not have any credit cards in his name but was a supplementary card holder who was partially responsible for the financial mess that had taken place. He simply blamed Bobby Dazzler for sucking the life out of the family money. Yet, once he left, it felt good and there was a sense of relief due to the peace and quiet that came after that. It felt as if a burden had been lifted. It was not meant to be, that is for sure. It was a matter of filing for divorce and moving on.

By September 2004, the Robson Street store was seized by bailiffs due to non-payment of rent for the past 3 months. The summer was clearly slow on Robson too. There was so many look-loos that rent was still just too high for the sales. This too felt great, as if another burden had been removed. Lucky for Bobby Dazzler, we maintained very low stock levels and much of the inventory had already been taken out of the store. The landlord was not going to let Bobby Dazzler go forever without paying rent. All that remained now was keeping the main "M" Mall store afloat until Halloween and Christmas so that some of the inventories could start to clear. So much for the dream of having a multi store operation. The debts were climbing sky high. To keep the store floating, lines of credit were secured because Christmas was coming. We needed a Christmas miracle. By the end of September, the children were moved from the family home to our own home away from the ex-hubby. A new start was needed. By late November 2004, the hoarding started to come down and the sales started to roll in. The outlook seemed a little better by the end of Christmas when this horrible year was coming to an end. Bills got paid, the financial mess seemed to clear due to being frugal and watching the money in a proper manner for the store to get off of the ground. Going into 2005, sales jumped every single month. A fresh breath of air seemed to come around for Bobby Dazzler. In late 2005, the landlord at "M" Mall was contacted in anticipation of getting a five plus five year lease. However, only a two-year extension was granted to Bobby Dazzler so that the mall was able to see how we would do after the renovation/construction/redevelopment was complete. It should be noted that according to British Columbia law, in order to sue the landlord for damages caused by the breach of contract that occurred during the redevelopment period, a plaintiff is allowed to sue within the two-year period. This was according to the Limitation Act. This was accepted since the lease was our livelihood and this store was the "bread and butter" of all stores. Bobby Dazzler hoped that after stellar sales, the landlord would be satisfied by the results and we would be able to continue with our business as usual. Bobby Dazzler moved forward personally, financially and in business in a positive direction. 2004 was a write-off year for sure or at least that is what we thought.

PIOTR

So, on February 21, 2005, a guy named Piotr walked into the "M" Mall Bobby Dazzler to purchase a Porsche key chain. Later, it would be found out that this is the very same Piotr that was read about in the local newspaper who was found with $800,000.00 in the trunk of his Porsche.

This client was very persistent about asking Bobby Dazzler out on a date. It was not uncommon in the retail world that clients asked the retail clerks out on dates. Sometimes, clients thought that there was more coming with the sale. It happened daily, not to boast. Many men would come and ask for dates before, during or after a purchase. This individual insisted. Piotr was a very nice guy at first just like everyone else who came into the store. He was polite and spoke nicely. He spoke a lot and revealed ALL his cards about himself, which should have been the clues as to who he really was. We went on a few dinner dates as friends but nothing substantial materialized. The relationship felt more business-like so we went down that road instead. Sometimes you have to take a chance. He seemed pretty smart with some money things and wanted to change his money situation around due to a job loss as a stockbroker. He had good drive so we decided that maybe we should do a project together.

At the time, the Vancouver real estate market was just picking up steam so a house renovation project seemed to be a good place to start. In late March 2005, I pointed out to Piotr a home on the North shore that could possibly be renovated and sold. The home was a fantastic deal; it was a foreclosure and needed fixing up. It could be a good home to flip. It was the LAST good deal in the neighborhood. We agreed to proceed with it as a business transaction. Everything was supposed to be 50/50. The down payment, renovations and mortgage payments were supposed to be shared equally in a partnership-like manner. Normally, two people are supposed to go on the mortgage but Piotr insisted that he take it out in his name only but he also had to be the sole owner; he insisted by stating just "stay out of it and trust me!" Piotr hadn't filled out his tax returns for the past three years but the bank we were dealing with was okay with the tax returns that he provided without any assessments. They could have been fakes as there was no way to determine if they were the ones that were filed. He provided an additional three years of returns previous to the tax returns that the bank was given and the bank approved the $700,000.00 mortgage. I had some credit card debts lingering for a poor 2004 and my credit rating would have dragged the deal down but we would have okay to have both of us on title. But, he really wanted it to be a solo thing. So, I let it be. I would be putting half the money in the down payment, closing costs and renovations by taking a huge risk and by trusting someone I had just met last month. Being a business woman means takings risks. In life we need to take risks, especially in business. He hadn't proven to me that I should doubt him yet. Yet, something obviously was off from that moment on. Given that this was supposed to be a 50/50 project, the mortgage and ownership should have been in both names. However, when closing time came, Piotr said that he did not have his half of the cash to close the deal. He needed to get an extension to get some more funds. Piotr indicated that he was going to a "buddy" to get some more cash. Bobby Dazzler already had our cash in order so now there were three options. We could either back away from the deal and lose the deposit, have Piotr come up with his half from elsewhere or we close using all of Bobby Dazzler's cash. Piotr came up with some more cash after claiming he tossed his Porsche off a cliff in Osoyoos, British Columbia in order to collect the insurance money. That didn't seem like the smartest thing to do plus it appeared to be a desperate move on his part. Was he kidding or was this real? I didn't buy that story. It became apparent that he not only did not have his portion of the down payment but also didn't have other funds for further renovations and mortgage payments. Piotr was counting on Bobby Dazzler's money to pull him through. Bobby Dazzler was not going to sink anymore money into the project until the house was under my name only not jointly. Not wanting to lose any more money meant that the home had to be transferred into Bobby Dazzler's name within two weeks. The point was to salvage the deal without taking a financial hit so that it could be renovated and sold. That was the original plan.

However, problems arose when it was discovered that Piotr was part of a very large police investigation. After doing a simple Google search of his name, it was discovered that Piotr was caught with $800,000 in his Porsche back in December 2002. The local Vancouver Sun ran the article. Oh no, this guy is a crook! Who the hell would put $800,000 in the trunk of their car and drive around downtown Vancouver. Right…or not! Perhaps this was Vancouver! Who would have ever thought that it was the same Piotr who would walk into Bobby Dazzler after reading about him in the newspaper a few years ago and thinking that this guy is crazy! Bobby Dazzler appeared to be a magnet for everybody and sometimes the crazy. It was probably the pink and blue neon lights around the store that drove them in.

Piotr had worked for a brokerage firm selling securities before being fired for the whole $800,000 in the Porsche trunk business/ fiasco. This new information obviously caused problems with our business deal. The police might think that Bobby Dazzler was involved or the house could become part of the investigation as it was still ongoing according to online stories. The house could be forfeited if police thought that Piotr used the proceeds of crime for it by mere association. Obviously, we needed to disconnect from Piotr as soon as possible. Subsequent Google searches linked him to some Vietnamese gangs who were caught money-laundering. Great, this is getting crazy fast, again! The deal would have been great, but now the truth had been revealed and it turned out to be not such a great deal It was too late to reverse the house renovation project but Piotr had other problems now. He did not have his share of funds. So how was he planning on doing this deal if he didn't have a job nor had any funds for a renovation?

Intuition revealed that it may have been Piotr's plan to bail the whole time. The home had to be transferred to Bobby Dazzler's name as no mortgage payments would be paid if he owned the home. The property transfer taxes had to be paid again in July 2005 within 2 weeks of the original purchase, by Bobby Dazzler since Piotr was not related. Bobby Dazzler demanded that this be the way the house project proceed. The bank was given notice that Piotr had no job and that the home was going to be transferred to Bobby Dazzler's name. Obviously, a fall-out was imminent. It took place after looking at all the funds that were sunk into the renovation project. Piotr started to get frustrated and wanted his portion of the funds which were only $20,000 out plus a whole lot extra which we did not agree on. After transferring the home, the threats and attempts to extort more money came. Piotr wanted $100,000, not his $20,000. Why? Because he saw the potential for profit? He sent letters via regular mail and then came letters from lawyers. Along with the letters came multiple tire-flattening episodes and the dead bird throws in mid-September 2005. Threats via email, phone, texts and even letters were normal for this guy. Well, it was time to call the cops, right?!?

Careful records were kept as all expenses for the home were being borne by Bobby Dazzler. There was no way to back out of this, now that so much money had been put into the house. Bobby Dazzler would have to pay him off but it wasn't going to be $100,000 for about two weeks of work and finding out that this guy was on the police radar. His intention was to squeeze money, Mafia style: extortion, business interference, threatening, racketeering and other organized crime activities that involved pushing people to the limit. He was a bully. Bobby Dazzler was only willing to give him roughly $24,000 at the time of closing that was put into the house. He was told to get a lawyer to deal with this properly. Unfortunately, that was not his style. Piotr started to stalk the Bobby Dazzler business and the house. It appeared that trouble had been bought. Since all the money was now sunk into this house, there was no choice but to move into it and do the renovation project slowly over time rather than it being a sale for flipping. After another flat tire in September 2005, the local police were called. The local police indicated that anything to do with Piotr was being handled by the Organized Crime Agency Special Enforcement Unit which is now called the Combined Forces Special Enforcement Unit. (CFSEU)

After calling the police, Sgt. Colin showed up at the store. Colin was given all the information of what had taken place. Sgt. Colin was told that Piotr even followed the ex-hubby and threatened him by saying that the "mob" was going to get my business and would harass me until I paid his $100,000. The ex-husband verified that he felt that Piotr indeed belong to the "mob" or some sort of organized group as he was an ex-military man himself from Israel and knew what this man was up to. The ex-hubby said that Bobby Dazzler should be careful as he seemed a little dangerous/off. This information was all passed along to Sgt. Colin of CFSEU and we were told to report all dealings, contact and information about Piotr or anybody else who might be connected to Sgt. Colin. However, no File # was ever given. Why was that the case? All interactions that took place with Piotr and all other suspicious people were to be reported Sgt. Colin via email so that a paper trail existed for all the communications that were provided to

CFSEU. That is exactly what Bobby Dazzler did for the next thirteen years. Yes, that is correct and not a typo! We even expressed our concerns that Piotr may have had something to do with us being thrown out of "M" mall. Sgt. Colin simply indicated that there were no connections whatsoever with this speculation. He pushed Bobby Dazzler not to believe that a connection existed. All emails from him just thanked us for the update. Sgt. Colin simply stated that maybe the people approaching us were just interested in our business. Well, we knew that already by this time. Bobby Dazzler was subjected to a significant amount of business interference, business racketeering, unnecessary audits and business problems/issues at the hands of the "mob" for the next 13 years. We were just a small retailer that sold a Porsche keychain from our store to the wrong guy, Piotr.

Piotr attempted to create money problems and financial chaos. Each time an audit took place, CRA asked Bobby Dazzler if we kept proper records. Each and every time the auditors found nothing. However, Piotr attempted to destroy Bobby Dazzler financially, somehow. He had CRA audit me in three separate types of audits in various departments including the Canada Border Services and the payroll. Our vehicle was subject to secondary searches each and every time it crossed the US border for stock and inventory. This resulted in long wait times, sometimes up to eight hours. Normally, the whole process is only a couple of hours. They all claimed to see if I had kept my records. Hence, he attempted to create havoc in the tax department by claiming that we didn't have records. Bobby Dazzler came out clean, each and every time.

After three years of wrangling back and forth with lawyers, a settlement was reached by January 2008 for around $60,000. However, during that time many more interesting characters showed up including an unusually high number of Iranian people who wanted to rent the basement suite of the home that was part of the renovation project that went sideways. There was no rhyme or reason for why this was going on until the plot thickened. One of them even asked if she could baby-sit the kids, even after not liking the basement suite. Weirdo! All contact information for each of these potential clients was kept, including names plus phone numbers. They all seemed suspicious. This was voiced to Sgt. Colin who also handled all the information. A formal settlement for the house came about, but not without a significant amount of damage being done to the Bobby Dazzler business at "M" Mall. Bobby Dazzler was not given a chance to renew at the "M" mall and a lawsuit was launched in 2007 due to sneaky and underhanded dealings which can be considered corruption. There was no contact with Piotr again till he called from Poland in October 2010 on my birthday. He admitted that he was the one who had us thrown out of "M" Mall as one of his contacts was Shawn, the GM (General Manager). He further claimed that his boss, who is an Iranian, wanted his money, the initial $24,000 plus interest back from him, but he had taken off to Poland due to the problems he was facing for causing the lawsuit at "M" Mall. Piotr told the Iranian boss that he had sunk the $24,000 into the house renovation and that he "should look for the 24K from me, with interest." Great, so Piotr basically got this man to come after me. This also explained the high number of high number of Iranians seeking to rent my basement suite. It should be pointed out that by this time Bobby Dazzler had met this boss that Piotr was talking about. Piotr even said that I should watch out for Iran and the Iranians as they control a lot of retail around town. The house was out of the picture and all documents pertaining to that had already been taken care of back in 2008. But having Piotr take responsibility for having the Bobby Dazzler business thrown out of "M" Mall also made the plot take a juicy twist. We met with Sgt. Colin 2010 to give a police lawyer the details of what was said by Piotr. We also asked why no File number was provided. Bobby Dazzler did not get a response back on this which made it appear as if Piotr may be part of CFSEU. Maybe a snitch?

What kind of clout does this boss have to be able to have a business thrown out of the mall for doing business with one of his employees, Piotr? Other than revenge, ego and the pure pursuit of throwing power around to give Piotr his $100K. It appeared that Piotr and his boss had contacts within the mall who may have believed what he was saying, but Piotr was just gossiping. There was never any truth in Piotr and his lies.

The question now remained as to who this contact was and what transpired as a result of *Sue'em* (short for sue them). Well, this Piotr fellow seemed to trigger a whole series of subsequent personally challenging events and conditions for Bobby Dazzler for years to come.

Shady

After Piotr, the shady characters just lined up one after another for years. After closing the store in "M" Mall, Bobby Dazzler removed a very large shell of an actual two-seat airplane that was hanging on the ceiling of the "M" Mall store as a prop. Having no room to display the airplane in the new location, Bobby Dazzler put the airplane up for sale on various websites like Craig'slist, Kijiji and Trade-a-plane. Suddenly, a dude by the name of Cham who claims to own an airport in the Valley calls up. He emails and indicates that he is interested in the plane. We arranged to meet at the storage unit that it was stored in and discussed it further and he appeared more interested in Bobby Dazzler. This guy didn't even end up being interested in the airplane. He asked why we weren't using it anymore and why we were not at "M" Mall anymore?

It is always interesting to make connections and usually the questions that a person asks lead to the real reason as to why they are even talking to you. Hmm, how do you know where it was hanging? I hadn't even said anything about that yet. This guy was just wasting my time. He was sent. I gave him my business card and said that if he knew anybody who wanted it then let them know where it can be found. After a couple days of he shows up at the store and asks if I want to have tea with him. Thinking that he changed his mind about purchasing the airplane, I accepted the invitation. While at tea, he probed again about why we aren't at "M" Mall. Bobby Dazzler was involved in a lawsuit by this time so it didn't seem like giving this guy information was the right thing to do plus it wasn't his business. Why was this guy even asking? What did he really want? After finishing up tea, he asked if I swam. This is a weird question?!? I said, "NO!" That is when he got even more suspicious. He asked if I wanted to go boating with him and meet a friend of his who is in the financial industry. This man must be crazy asking me onto a boat after asking if I swim. Upon my return back to the store, an email was sent to Sgt. Colin again, outlining the details of this encounter and that it was strange, with the possibility of it being connected to Piotr. All that arrived from him was another, "thank you for the update." Don't the cops want this guy's name, phone number and more details to question him? This Cham guy was definitely shady! As time went on, the shady guys came one by one into the store by calling, emailing or just accidental run-ins at the trade shows. I googled his name and he did indeed hold a boating license since they show online who took the lessons along with pass dates. The coincidence about this was that Scott, another supplier of Bobby Dazzler, also happened to take the boating lessons with Cham. Well, that puts two and two together.

After going to a trade show in Vegas, Gord, a supplier friend of mine, says the owner of another retail store wants to meet you. "Why, Gord?" He says, "I don't know but he asked to be introduced to you." I gave the aisle number I would be in and the time, so we get introduced to each other. Well, it turned out be yet an Iranian man and this one wanted to know if the Bobby Dazzler business was for sale right now. This was getting too crazy for me. I just said "no" and the reason it wasn't was due to the fact that the lawsuit was underway, so Bobby Dazzler just walked away from this guy named Razi. He then left a message at the hotel I was staying in, asking to meet for dinner. After calling him and asking him how he found out which hotel I was staying in, he said Gord told him. But this was still creepy! I wasn't interested in meeting up with this dude, especially in Vegas. G-d knows what his intentions were. Plus there was no need to, after the whole airplane incident with Cham.

Just after that guy was dealt with, a supplier buddy from a long time ago coincidentally runs into Bobby Dazzler in the exact same aisle that I was in at the Vegas trade show, at 9:15 am, the next day. It was the same Scott that took those boating lessons with Cham, the airplane man. Scott made it appear that it was a coincidence but it didn't feel like it since there are 5,000+ exhibitors at the show with over 150 aisles. Was Scott the next shady dude?

Shawn

We will get to Scott once we are done with Shawn. Shawn was the person in charge of "M" Mall but he was not the Leasing Manager. We rubbed each other the wrong way and he wasn't supposed to be dealing with leases. He had only arrived at the complex two years before. Shawn would be a problem as he made some rude comments to me in the loading bay area, giving me his true inner spirit. I recalled ignoring him and knew he was on a high horse. Immature and amateur were only two words. Who would have known that guy was going to be given so much power over our future here at "M" Mall. Shawn's comment would further lead to his deciding our faith, livelihood, and future in the center he managed. It was obvious that Bobby Dazzler would be pushed out, as all independent retailers were systematically being pushed out in favor of big business, nationals and FASHION. Well, Shawn was certain that he was going to do this somehow. Shawn was in his late twenties or early thirties. As time went on, it appeared that someone had paid him handsomely to ensure that Bobby Dazzler would not be around.

By 2007, Bobby Dazzler had cornered the novelty/giftware industry. We were the only ones doing what we were doing and were making a lot of money doing so. Others wanted to jump in on it but who? Shawn indicated a competitor and The Sharper Image were looking for spots. But the competitor had ready been here, done that and left in 2003. The Sharper Image was not expanding to Canada. This guy was bullshitting me. So why would they even entertain competitors? They were big and so was the landlord. The rather large usually like to do business with the large. Why wouldn't the landlord want us to stay in the mall? We had a proven track record and also we were promised a lease after the two year wait-and-see period was up. Shawn made it appear that he wasn't interested in having little local, independent retailers from British Columbia around when he could get the large in. The large like to scratch the backs of the large. They could ensure that this was going to help the both of them. However, there was something off with his tone and his mannerism.

After speaking to the area manager of the competitor, they indicated they had no interest in returning to this mall. They referred the mall to as "mental town" due to the high theft rate and low sales rate. The same landlord owned three other major malls so they had a sole monopoly on the great mall real estate. This prevented us from obtaining a spot in the other malls because big business ensures that big business will get larger along with them. Those other spots would be waiting for a competitor, not for Bobby Dazzler. They would never even come up with offers to us.

After putting our proper notice to renew in late 2006 after a couple of very, very successful Christmas selling seasons, Bobby Dazzler felt certain that a long-term lease would be provided. After all, we had been in the mall for almost 17 years and expressed a strong desire to the maintain status quo. Shawn responded to our letter by having his assistant call the store. He did not respond via written communications. She indicated Shawn would have some time to see us on this or that day. Shawn must have liked his power and his position in the mall, as previous GM's just came down to speak to us or called personally. So on December 15, 2006, I received a call that Shawn would like to meet with me on January 15, 2007 to discuss my letter for request of a renewal. So when January 15 rolled around, we met, along with Paula who was the leasing manager. I pointed out that our store was number one or two in sales reporting for December for our category despite the fact that my neighbor, a dentist, was allowed to proceed with a renovation in the mall during Christmas. I felt that it was ridiculous to allow this nuisance to occur. Shawn, pretending to be ignorant, simply stated that we have some great shopping days coming ahead so go for it. Shawn said that he felt that Bobby Dazzler should be in the "EE" zone. The "EE" was the entertainment zone. In our eyes, "EE" meant extra empty not E for entertainment. There was nothing entertaining in the "EE" zone. He felt we were a destination store which did not need walk-by traffic. He was attempting to put us into the failed, old competitor's local: a location that they left as it was not busy. Everybody needs walk by traffic; every retailer knows that. Anybody who has a super-good concept needs to be found. LOCATION, LOCATION, LOCATION is NOT a made up concept by retailers. Foot traffic is necessary to survive and tenants must pay for this not just for the image or advertising but for sales. It become clear this guy had no idea where he got his schooling from. Location was important, especially to our business. Bobby Dazzler was a bling, bling retailer that is in your face and wants to be seen with a bam. What the hell is going on here. Every retailer in the world is aware that

"Location, Location" is of utmost importance and the most important word of retail space. Shawn gave us a couple of options, both in the "E" zone. Neither of the options were as great.

It was time to think and request a better location. All of this was put forth in a letter on February 5th, 2007. No response was provided when calls were made to Paula and Shawn; they just ignored me. Meanwhile, Shawn got the accountant to request an audit of our sales. My lease had a clause in it that said that if upon an audit my sales were under-reported by 3% than the mall could give a 30 day notice to terminate. 3% is such a minor percentage that even a little off could cause the landlord to act in a heavy handed-manner which, in the opinion of Bobby Dazzler, the landlord was doing. Were they trying to get me out? So, after a month of going through my books, they came out clean. The margin of error was only 1.5%. Whatever! Bobby Dazzler wrote another letter to leasing on March 5th requesting a response and confirming that the audit revealed nothing out of the ordinary. Paula called and said the entire lease-renewal process was being decided upon by Shawn. This is when the red flags went off. Shawn was not the leasing manager. They simply put all this situation in the hands of Shawn. What a nightmare; this one guy has sole responsibility to do what he wants, when he wants and with whom he wants. There is far too much room for corruption, disaster, disorder, chaos and the possibility of unethical business dealings. This was just asking for a sue'em situation, which Bobby Dazzler would prepare for diligently. Shawn held another meeting with me on March 22 without ever giving any written documentation, this time pointing out that NOT very many options were available for me to choose from, and the meeting to EE19 being the only choice for me to go to. EE19 was the former location of the competitor and they left it due to it being unsuccessful. Well, that would have to do if it was the only spot. We knew that Shawn was trying to make a fool out of us. Bobby Dazzler asked him to send the offer. He agreed and said that he would send an offer by email. Needless to say, NO offer came by April 1, 2007. I wrote again, indicating how well my sales were in March 2007. Shawn emailed me indicating that he was about to put together an offer but felt there was no point. What do you mean, NO POINT?

By this time all conversations were being recorded. All of the conversations with Shawn were being recorded with my tape recorder in my purse. It had to be done this way, as this guy was unwilling to give me anything in writing. Bobby Dazzler wanted to make sure that he was indeed offering us a location and not just wasting our time. After that meeting, Bobby Dazzler called the District Manager of "M" Mall in order to go over Shawn's head and it was discovered that EE19 was not even available from the get-go. This is fraud! Shawn was attempting to offer EE19 in hopes that we would say NO to a spot that didn't even work for our competitor. However, Bobby Dazzler was desperate to secure a spot. He was attempting to illegally email me an offer via email when it was a legal and binding document that needed to be put forth in written, fax, or hard copy form that is normally sent by hand through security, mail, registered mail or courier. These were clearly unfair dealings and obviously unethical. Bobby Dazzler knew this as it was clearly stated in the lease and that is the manner that previous and all leases had been dealt with. Additionally, the normal practice of sending an offer requires the landlord to send three copies of the offer plus a blank form of the lease so that a tenant has the ability to read it over before signing. Shawn felt as if he was dealing with a rookie and thought we would believe the landlord would send "real" offers in this form. This is when that course on lease law came in handy and the textbooks were still around from Simon Fraser University. You just never know when you can use it. Shawn may have thought if he could email me a ridiculous offer that I would simply reject his offer to lease in email form and nobody would ever know since it was in email form that could be deleted. Shawn was mistaken.

Bobby Dazzler enjoyed a very unique position in the retailer sector of novelties. We had ousted the likes of competitors, Gizmos, San Francisco Gifts, and Glow. We were the one and only, so we were willing to go anywhere it was available. We were willing to fight for our business. All the landlord had to do was offer the space. Bobby Dazzler knew the landlord had space but just didn't want to offer it for some reason and it was starting to feel a little stinky around here. All our clients and those who were looking for our products would find us no matter where we were going to be. We put forth that Bobby Dazzler would go as low as 800 square feet or as high as 2000 square feet so left the square-footage requirement wide open. However, we need a spot among the 550+ units that were in "M" Mall. Please provide us a spot. NO can do! Something didn't feel right anymore. The lease negotiations were not feeling fair. It may be the owner (landlord), the staff, the crook - OC (Organized Crime) or large business (competitor) but something didn't feel right. Was Bobby Dazzler making far too much money for someone's liking? We had to report sales so the mall knew. Shawn did not like it, our competitor did not like it, who else did not like it?

As mentioned earlier, it is difficult to do business as a woman and being singled out again in this process did not help. Why was this guy not giving us a proper written document with an offer? What the hell is going on here? Bobby Dazzler felt that we being targeted. Could this be another case of bribes that goes along with the business of this sort? This was clearly small-minded thinking. The righteous should prevail. Bobby Dazzler stayed quiet and watched until the time came to punch hard in the face. Watch out! Shawn was not giving a chance for this long-term independent tenant to renew when they had the ability to do so. The mall simply had NO room for a single woman of visible minority, who actually created a fantastic concept that the malls didn't have. It just became another constant lifelong battle of large business attempting to block a liberal, creative retailer who brought diversity to the mall.

After contacting Teddy, the district manager, we were told a mistake had been made. Well, Shawn was just trying to make us look like fools. This was not a mistake, it was intentional. That spot was offered from January 2007 to April 2007 and he was not under duress when he offered it. Bobby Dazzler made it clear that we would be able to renovate and pay the higher rent. We also mentioned to the landlord that since Bobby Dazzler would be relocating within the same center, the landlord was supposed to pay for the relocation as stated in the current lease. There was a clause in the current lease that specifically stated this. Well, why should we pay for your lack of planning, your unwillingness to cooperate, and honor the lease clause? The clause in the lease was clear. The landlord was supposed to pay for the relocation. This is when Teddy phones and says that we don't have a spot in our center, Bobby Dazzler. All spots are leased out or spoken for. Just like that we were told to go. There was no need to move our store in the first place. Why would we need to be moved when we agreed to whatever rent the mall wanted in the current location? The landlord was avoiding its clause in the lease to pay for a new location in the center by simply stating they didn't have a unit available. Additionally, if they planned a move, they should be able to come up with a location equal in size or similar in size so our business would NOT be adversely affected. But the mall just simply did not care and completely disregarded our plea. We just wanted a lease. EE19 would have been fine but the mall is supposed to pay for the move since we are NOT new tenants. We are re-locating within the same complex and it was clearly stated in our lease. They did NOT want to, so they decided to come up with anything to PUSH us out or at least come up with a reason. A reason in retail is called a breach of the lease. This time it wasn't Bobby Dazzler who breached the lease.

For the next couple of months, crazy requests started to come in. Clients looking for such items as sling shots, guns, knives, bear spray, stun-guns, tasers etc. We did sell them in prior years in our locations and knew that the lease forbade it. These are all items that are banned and cannot be sold according to this lease. They are all military items which is contrary to the lease. Teens started coming in and attempted to purchase rolling papers. This too is against the law. Minors are NOT allowed to purchase rolling papers. When it become clear that all of the requests that came in would lead to a breach of the lease, we were able to put two and two together. These requests were coming from the landlord who knew they were wrong to not have us moved to another location at their expense. They were simply attempting to find us in breach of our lease. The mall was trying anything they could to prove that we were doing something illegal. Thus, a breach or default would occur. Additionally, the landlord sent some of their friends in so that they could see if we carried items that would be considered a nuisance to the mall. Some items that they were looking for were bongs, dildos, sniffers (bullets), or even guns. Well, we weren't carrying any of those items but rumors were beginning to circulate in the complex that Bobby Dazzler was a dealer. Sure, it may have appeared as though we were, as the type of clients that we drew were from those circles, but we were just retailers not dealers. Our clients had money and we were there to take the money. There was nothing else going on at Bobby Dazzler other than retailing. There were no hookers hooking out the back door nor was weed being sold from the stockroom. Everybody suddenly came up with stories about what Bobby Dazzler was up to. We became a heat score all of a sudden. In the last two and half months leading to the end of August, the requests got crazier until we started to kick out people with attitude. We were specialty retailers of gifts, gadgets, novelties, and licensed merchandise. Shawn could not cover his tracks, his mistakes, and his lack of planning, so attempted to make us look like bad. Well, the landlord would get our ultimate notice shortly as we felt that Shawn had screwed up. Bobby Dazzler was not going to pay for this screw-up or lack of planning. We did want others to know just how unfairly we were treated. Bobby Dazzler just completed its two most successful years. Net income was at the best level. There had to be some smoke and fire in this mess that Shawn created. Bobby Dazzler didn't mind ruffling some feathers

After Bobby Dazzler left "M" Mall and the Notice of Claim was filed, Shawn suddenly left the mall and transferred to the Middle East to a Dubai mall. Well, isn't that a quinky dink! It was our suspicions and speculation the whole time that Shawn was acting in concert with and under the direction of team Iran or Piotr. We were not going to sit around and do nothing, Bobby Dazzler was going to sue'em. We were going to try to get justice either through a lawsuit or through a book that would reveal what it was like to do business in malls with a large landlord. Shawn represented the landlord and would have to answer all that had occurred in the last few months leading up the demise of Bobby Dazzler in "M" Mall.

After leaving Shawn's office in April 2005, Bobby Dazzler got two very unusual emails on the 26th of April at around 1:46am and 1:50am. They read as follows:

The first read: subject disabled

Message: see

The second email read: you

Message: office

This message was kept of course in my emails.

Well, the only time Bobby Dazzler was ever in an office this year and felt disabled was with Shawn during our meeting on March 22, 2006. Shawn just wasn't able to find space for Bobby Dazzler among 550 stores. Would Shawn really have the gall to send this email? Well, we would have see how this turned out in *Sue'em* as that is what we did in October 2007.

LEASE

The lease is the most important document for retail. Without a lease, there is no retail business. The lease is ironclad and generally favors the landlord. The lease is a document that is part of the retail jail as it is so very hard to break out of if the business is not doing well. The lease needs to be signed by the corporate officers of the company if the company is a limited company or it must be signed by the owners of a proprietorship or partnership. Bobby Dazzler signed its first lease in 1990. The landlord knew that I was young with a new concept but believed in us at the time. The landlord at the time provided our business with a very generous leasehold improvement allowance. This is a per square foot allowance that is provided to a new tenant for use to build the unit that is being leased to the liking of the tenant and landlord specs. Our store was over 1600 sq. ft. and this landlord provided it to us at $75 per square. Wow! That was a very generous amount for 1990. But, we were signing a five plus five year lease with an option to renew along with agreeing to sign a personal guarantee.

A personal guarantee protects the landlord should the tenant default on rent or breach the lease. It enables the landlord to pursue the tenant on a personal basis. This can be a scary document to sign but at the age of 19 there was nothing to lose. The owner was too young to own any major assets so we signed. The landlord required that we provide them with a guarantee of some sort so they would be protected should the business fail. So they asked us to sign a personal guarantee that the rents would be paid by requiring personal indemnification. The only problem was that Bobby Dazzler was only 19 and didn't have any assets other than all funds that were being sunk into the retail business. They wanted someone else, older. We needed to find another person who would be willing to put his or her name on a legal document that gave the landlord the power to come after them if the Bobby Dazzler business failed. Who in their right mind would be willing to take a chance on a 19 year old with an idea? The financial partner indicated that he had a 82 year old grandmother in a hospice who had signed all her financial affairs to her family already, who might be the best person. He wondered if she would do it and if the landlord would agree. This sounded a little off, to get an elderly person to sign. I didn't know if she had assets or not but we needed this deal to go through. The landlord agreed thinking that this person definitely had more assets than the 19 year old. Bobby Dazzler made the lease indemnification work.

By the time the lease came up for renewal in 1995, the landlord knew that we had accumulated assets since we were doing great. They requested that Bobby Dazzler personally sign the lease this time. Having no choice at the time, Bobby Dazzler transferred all cash, cars and personal real estate into her mother's name, to protect them.. Even though the store was doing great, there was no way that anybody should take a chance at losing the shirt off their back. Having watched some retailers in the mall lose everything including their house due to a failed business meant that it is better to take the shrewd and cautious path than to be reckless. Thus, we were able to sign indemnification agreements in the future, knowing that personal assets were protected in our mother's name.

The Bobby Dazzler business was doing phenomenally as some of its competitors decided to exit the mall prior to the major renovations, redevelopment or extra-long construction that was upcoming for 2004-2006. In fact, Bobby Dazzler had cornered the market by around this time. Since the Bobby Dazzler business had been in the complex for so many years we felt that it would be a shoe-in to get another lease in the same unit or elsewhere in this complex that would soon to have 550 units. We had paid a few million dollars in rent and were not bad tenants. The landlord was called and proper documents were sent in late December 2004 for a renewal. However, a lease extension for two years was given on the premise that sales were so dismal at the time that the landlord needed to see just how renovation/ redevelopment had impacted the Bobby Dazzler business.

Notes to the documents were made:
- A lease and particularly a commercial one is a contract that builds an ongoing relationship (as opposed to a single, isolated transaction)
- Since both parties are aware that a business has put its name, leasehold improvements, and livelihood in a location in a mall, the landlord is in the position of continuing the relationship so long as both parties are in agreement and are NOT in default or breach of each other.

- It is important to remember that the relationship is an on-going one between the landlord and tenant which this was, as it had been many years since 1990. The tenant wrote in a timely manner to ensure that this relationship would continue as the business, reputation, and livelihood of our business was at stake.
- A lease defines the parameters of a relationship of close de facto co-operation that can last for years, i.e., 1990-1995 one five-year term, another five-year term provided 1995-2000, yet another five-year term provided 2000-2005, then an extension provided for two years to prove that an ongoing relationship was occurring with the landlord.
- If the landlord was not satisfied with the tenant then three five-year terms would not have been given

The landlord gave Bobby Dazzler a two-year extension at the end of the day due to the fact that they wanted to see what would happen to our sales since they had tanked due to the redevelopment that was taking place. By 2006, the biggest turnaround in sales took place. The sales were better than they were prior to the renovation and redevelopment of the mall. Bobby Dazzler gave proper notice in 2006 that we would like to have another five year lease with an option to renew for another five years. This notice was given in December 2006 when we saw the great profits and sales. This just meant that we would need to do another negotiation within two years. But other events and characters would come in to Bobby Dazzler to make this story even more sensational and show what type of retail jail came about. This was discussed in *Shawn*.

SUE'EM

Sue'em is the abbreviation of "sue them" and in the business world, it is a common term. It was once said that suing is one of America's favorite pastimes. Maybe that is why we have so many lawyers. When doing business, there is something that can go wrong which does and sometimes the other party just does not feel responsible for the actions that led to the problem. That is when one sues another or gets sued for financial compensation. This process involves the court, a judge and some lawyers. It is not only a very expensive process that only the rich or wealthy are able to afford but it is a process that many will say one should steer clear of. But what if a true wrong has taken place? What about justice? Sue'em may be the only recourse. The matter is then put forth in front of the court system so that the judge will be able to decide what the outcome will be. Really, it is something that one should never be afraid of so long as one responds to the writ of summons that goes along with this. In the end, the claim is either thrown out, settled, or reduced. Sue'em is not a big deal. Most people are scared of the courts but the courts have real people in them too. If you are right and need to proceed in this manner, just say as it is. Present the case and see what happens.

So, like any small business, Bobby Dazzler had to sue'em several times. But, the "big" sue'em that would become most interesting was the one that took place in 2007 just after dealing with Shawn and can be found under File# S076921 which was filed at the Vancouver Registry. This lawsuit was filed against the landlord at "M" Mall that happened to be a very large institutional investor that managed several public pension plans and insurance programs in Quebec. Among the main depositors of this institution were many different government employee retirement plans and various government agencies.

By going into the Court Registry, Bobby Dazzler filed a claim and sued under the Limited company's name. Some business buddies suggested that Bobby Dazzler leave this one alone and move on with the business in our new location that was in a suburban mall just outside of Vancouver in "C" Center. They even said that you should watch out since you are dealing with a very large Goliath who has many connections and it could essentially be the Government. This same company also owned five other malls that were in the Greater

Vancouver area so it wasn't like we could just pick up and go to another one of their busy malls. Bobby Dazzler felt that an injustice had take place so we decided to pursue it. Plus, if we didn't get justice then how would we know, learn from the process, and the lessons could never be shared. Sharing of information enables others to learn from this retail experience. This was our retail experience and our experience with suing them.

So, from 2007 to 2009, a number of individuals came along that became annoying, shady characters due to the lawsuit being filed. There was Piotr, Scott, Cham, Razi, Saied, and Sgt. Colin. Bobby Dazzler didn't hang with any of these people but suddenly they wanted to hang with Bobby Dazzler and to join their "inner circle" as Scott put it.

Scott, a Bobby Dazzler supplier/wholesaler, would show up at the Trade Shows in Las Vegas in the same exact row that Bobby Dazzler was going through, supposedly looking for products in a coincidental manner. There is absolutely no way that individuals could bump into each other at a Trade Show that had 5,000 exhibitors. Creep is the only word for this guy. Most people either go to the left or the right when they start to walk the floor looking for products at 9 am. Bobby Dazzler would go to the middle due to less traffic and there was Scott at the Las Vegas Trade show in the exact same row that Bobby Dazzler would start in. All the way from Vancouver. This was just weird. He asked if I wanted to join him for a show or dinner. I thought as any nice person would and said sure, just to find out what he wanted! At this time, Bobby Dazzler had already started to take notes of the issues to compile this memoir. Bobby Dazzler wanted more juicy stuff. His main topic was business and selling the business. He emphasized it and instilled the idea in each of his sentences. He actually said it about three times. Sure, Bobby Dazzler can put some thought into that idea.

After getting back to Canada, on many occasions not only would Scott send many invites to his home parties which would be highly suspicious since we never were friends and never had that sort of a relationship before. This happened on a weekly basis since filing the claim in October 2007 and onwards. Taking him up on couple of the offers proved to be exactly what was expected of this individual. He was observed pouring some funky liquid into the red wine that was being served to his guests at his condo located in Yaletown, Vancouver, at one of his parties. Upon taking a quick sip, those suspicions proved to be true. Thankfully, I had arrived with a friend named Sally, not alone of course. I told her what I saw and tasted. We got out of his party very quickly. Since everything that Scott was doing was very suspicious, his activities were also reported to Sgt. Colin. It was even stated that Scott may be following Bobby Dazzler around at the Las Vegas trade show. Sgt. Colin insisted that he might just want to do business with us. A quick Google search revealed that Cham, the shady guy who wanted to take me on a boat did boating lessons with the same Scott that was inviting me to his parties. This was not a coincidence. It was putting two and two together.

The response that was received was surprising to say the least. Sgt. Colin stated that he may be keeping his business options open. It should be noted that Sgt. Colin who represents the police did say that any or all suspicious contact relating to Piotr should be reported to him. This was done via written communications via email. Something was definitely amiss with the response received by Colin. It was also pointed out to Sgt. Colin that Bobby Dazzler felt that Piotr had something to do with what happened to Bobby Dazzler at the "M" Mall. Sgt. Colin pushed all this information under the carpet, indicating that there was no connection to Piotr and "M" Mall but he would keep his eyes/ears open. All this information was provided as requested to Colin via email from 2007 onwards.

Additional problems arose at the new location which was in another mall. Resumes would arrive with no address, part-time staff would be hired who worked inefficiently, strange individuals would come in the store to videotape the store without permission, clients would make purchases then demand unreasonable refunds, a higher than normal rate of items committing suicide off the shelves occurred, theft rose to an all-time high and issues with the new landlord (owner) arose. Letters telling Bobby Dazzler not to display this item or that t-shirt in the window became a daily occurrence. This also included some merchandise all of a sudden being unsuitable for sale, despite the lease specifically stating that Bobby Dazzler was allowed to sell it. Essentially, so many nuisances were being created that anybody in their right mind would want to get the hell out of the retail store or just sell it. The accounting department stating that they were not receiving the monthly sales reports on time and also the landlord indicating that they had not received the "Annual Audited Statement of Sales" for years 2007 and 2008 when they were hand delivered and emailed in a timely manner for those years. These were important documents since they allowed the landlord to terminate the lease due to non-receipt of it within a 30-day time frame according to the lease. It appeared the landlord started to give Bobby Dazzler the same problems that were experienced over at the "M" Mall store. Someone was going through the lease with a fine-toothed comb to come up with something to get rid of Bobby Dazzler. All of a sudden, the tax audits started up again by the provincial and governmental authorities. Inspections by the local bylaw officers increased up along with "surprise" inspections by the fire department, the tobacco officers who came by the store despite there being no tobacco products in the store, the WCB (Work Safe) people to see if we were registered or not. This was just like in the movie, *Godfather*. The authorities were used to get rid of the competitor or a competing business. Laws in the United States do exist to prevent this from happening. That is anti-racketeering laws. But, not in good old safe Canada. The wealthy Iranian group could take over businesses and cause a lot of nuisance if they have the "right people in their back pocket," which it appeared to in the eyes of Bobby Dazzler.

Bobby Dazzler was prepared, as we had just gone through the exact same scenario at the "M" Mall business. It was simply a continuation of more problems in order to bring Bobby Dazzler down or to have it kicked out of the mall. This happened during the course of two years while lawsuit while it awaited a trial date. Of course, nothing ever happened since we were in compliance with every single aspect of our business.

The lawsuit continued and it went to Summary Trial in November 2009. During the time leading up to the trial, the above events took place sometimes weekly but definitely monthly.

After spending about $30k on a lawyer and not happy with his work, Bobby Dazzler self-represented. At trial, Bobby Dazzler self-represented but with some coaching done by David (a former lawyer) and the Defendant was represented by Susan. The trial took an entire day to go through but took about five-six days for the Judge to come up with a final decision. Of course, the Defendants offered a low ball amount of $5,000 as settlement so that I would not have to pay for costs that could have been double costs for the company. However,

Bobby Dazzler refused since that is not the amount of loss that we had experienced. We were entitled to a lease. We asked for $1.2 million since we were expecting a 10-year lease as promised by the landlord when the major renovations and redevelopment of the entire store took place in 2004/2005. This $1.2 represented the amount of total losses including wages and profits for a 10 year period. The landlord did not agree to this amount. Bobby Dazzler felt that the landlord (owner) had reneged on their promise plus fraudulently offered a space that was not available along with not paying for the relocation as the lease had stated. This was not fair nor proper business. Additionally, the landlord chose to play games with Bobby Dazzler by offering a spot for four months that belonged to a former competitor but wasn't even available from the get-go. $5,000 was simply not enough to settle on since it also meant that Bobby Dazzler would not have been able to discuss this case if the $5,000.00 was accepted. With a settlement of such a small amount, Bobby Dazzler would not be able to disclose what took place in our retail story. It was better to forgo the $5,000 than to accept it, as others would never be helped or made aware as to what can happen to small retailers when dealing with the Goliath of a landlord.

SMASH

After filing the lawsuit in October 2007, it felt as if everybody wanted to smash the Bobby Dazzler business. This word became significant as time went on and as personal challenges in retail intensified. The lawsuit seemed to bring on a whole new set of problems that never really existed before. Maybe the problems were tied to Piotr and his threats but new characters came into play, and it felt like they were working in conspiracy to sabotage the Bobby Dazzler business.

After opening for business in "C" Center in September 2007, a crew of one General Manager, one Retail Manger and two lawyers came into the store at the end of November to check out our entire store operation including every single item that we sold. This was unusual as we had never experienced this in any one of our locations. A subsequent visit in December 2007 arrived whereby we were asked to open up all the cupboards under the smoking section to determine if "other" products or "stuff" was being sold. What was going on? Some naughty t-shirts were pulled from being displayed and then a stockroom inspection took place. Of course, nothing was found.

Smash is a unique word! Only Piotr has used it. Going through business courses in university and in high school helped Bobby Dazzler to understand what the word smash means. After the lawsuit was filed in October 2007, individuals, companies and businesses that were related to the credit card business, the debit/credit card processing business, third party credit card processors and other business finance companies approached Bobby Dazzler via oral/verbal communications, personal in-store visits and via written communications through email or mail. Each and every single one of these companies required us to consent to a credit check or pulling of a credit report. Bobby Dazzler firmly believed that these companies' constant ongoing attempts to obtain our credit report was related to the lawsuit that was most recently filed in October 2007. We never had any companies from these sectors approach us before.

A corporate lawyer friend indicated that at times companies being sued sometimes approach these companies to determine the financial health of the company or individual who is suing them. This made sense as any large company would want to know who is suing them and a credit report can paint the picture well for any company. So, this explained the constant attempts to obtain a copy of the credit report for Bobby Dazzler. The only problem was that this continued for ten years even after the lawsuit had gone to trial in 2009.

Companies even approached Bobby Dazzler so much that we got an answering machine to screen our calls and not answer the phone anymore. We would never answer a number we didn't recognize or know. Large business started to approach Bobby Dazzler to agree to the Terms and Conditions along with their Privacy Policy for the next ten years. Deep inside the legal jargon the Terms and Conditions plus the Privacy Policy was CONSENT. This is a legally binding agreement if clicked by an individual or company to give consent to whichever company that click was made for to obtain private, confidential and personal information on an individual or a company. Many people often click the Terms and Conditions of a company policy without ever reading it or even knowing what they are agreeing to. This is important not just in the online retail world since almost all businesses have some sort of privacy policy or Terms and Conditions of doing business with them. This is sometimes confusing to the consumer, a retailer or regular person who in most instances does not read the Terms and Conditions but simply clicks. Consent to view one's private banking information and/or pull a credit report can have serious ramifications for an individual or company if they are suing a large company or if an enemy has been made along the way in the business world.

Information about such can be harmful especially in business when it is so easy to have conflict, friction and disagreements related to the retail world or any business world whether they are related or not. It our case we had friction with "M" Mall and Piotr which Bobby Dazzler believed to be related. It can used as a way to "smash" a business if someone really wanted to. That is where smash came to be for Bobby Dazzler. In fact, Bobby Dazzler even read an article on Piotr in the Vancouver Sun that indicated that many different avenues or contacts are used by governmental agencies in order to obtain information. By mere association with Piotr, we felt that we may have been targeted for many years of this smash.

Scott

Scott is was known as Mr. Quote man. We could have done a lot more business over the number of years that we had known each other but it just never happened that way. We were both local Vancouverites who had so much in common with respect to the type of business that we were involved in but the numbers and sales with each other just never took off. However, there was something strange about Scott. Really strange, if my mom picked up on it. After coming along with me to a Gift Show in Vancouver once, she shook his hand and said, "your hands are really sweaty" to his face. I was embarrassed and so was Scott. But she just blurted out what she thought and later said I don't recommend trusting that guy, Scott. Basically, Scott was a local wholesaler of virtually all of the products that we sold but something about the way he did things made Bobby Dazzler not have such a close relationship nor do mass amounts of business with him. It might even have ended with him accusing us of damaging a product called plasma ball after reporting it as defective when it arrived at our store. We didn't need this as our American suppliers took our word for it or simply wanted us to send them a picture of the broken or defective item for a credit or just believed us if we said a damaged item arrived. But generally, they took our word for it.

So, it was really strange when Scott started to phone us out of the blue in 2007 to say he was going to drop by in late August and do a sales call. He dropped by, appeared pleasant. He asked why I didn't buy more from him. The short answer was that his prices were higher than the American suppliers that we had lined up. In September, he suddenly emailed asking if I would be available to do lunch. This was kind of odd as we never had really done this type of thing in the past, except once when he offered to do a joint project with him along with another buddy. However, we passed due to the trust issues with this dude and nothing seemed really sincere with him. After ignoring the first email, he sent another in mid-September claiming he was doing a lunch for all his friends who are Libras in October and wanted me to come. It was out of the blue, unusual, out of the ordinary and not very normal for him to just call and want to do lunch. We never did this before so why now? After asking the questions, "What is it that you need?" and "What is it that you want?" Bobby Dazzler became interested and wanted to find out what he wanted. He dropped by the store to see if I had made up my mind about the lunch. He brought a gift and was insistent. Then, he asked if I wanted to go for a drink and I thought, why not? Well, I am writing this reveal all and needed some juicy stuff to write about. We met across the street and chatted for about 45 minutes. He asked a couple of direct questions which were kind of giving me the idea that someone had sent him to ask me what I was up to. What is it that I do? How do I make money? What do I do with my time? These are all weird questions as I owned Bobby Dazzler, made money from it and all my time was spent doing this. He indicated that he did these lunches with people all the time: networking lunches to connect people together. It seemed like he was fishing or perhaps to get reaction out of me.

Scott wanted to find out what I did for a living. I thought that we both knew what I did. Remember, I was a retailer and he was a wholesaler. His inquisitive questions only proved what I had always thought of him. Kind of weird! I told him that reading and writing are fun as pastimes. The blah, blah, and blahs went on a bit and some more bullshit with icing on the top! He said that he was doing some business in Thailand with Hells Angels. Yah, sure! Nobody drops things like that to a casual friend. I thought this guy was full of shit. Well, good for you! Then, all of a sudden after only one drink, Scott had to go quickly. That was the weirdest meeting that I ever had with a person attempting to get some information. Before leaving, he then indicated that he wanted me to join his inner circle of friends and have lunch with some really cool other Libras next month. Scott sort of insisted and said that someone wanted to meet me. I accepted and wondered again what all this was about! I guessed we would find out sooner rather than later.

At the lunch, we met with a bunch of men. They were all pleasant and nice! I only knew Scott and was introduced to three others who were all sitting down before I got there. They all were into the financial or investment banking types of businesses. Interesting! Why am I here? I am just a retailer. Anyway, Scott said the man who wants to meet you is on his way. After about 10-15 minutes, an Iranian man sits down next to me and gives me his business card. His name is Saied. He owns a currency exchange around town. After putting two and two together,

I started to think that guy is the "Boss" that Piotr may have been working for and told me about. Wait, this might be the guy that Piotr borrowed money from. Maybe?!? We finished lunch and then departed by exchanging business cards and cell phone numbers. There wasn't any harm in doing that plus I would love to explain what Piotr had said if it should ever come up. Saied asked if I could give him a ride back to his business. I said, "Sure!" He pointed to a small currency exchange on the street and said that dinky, money exchange business is his. But, he said it without really moving his mouth and almost sarcastically. This was NOT his only business. When someone makes it seem that they are just a small, little guy then usually they are BIG! That came from watching many gangster movies. So, Scott put me in touch with Saied.

Saied

Scott introduced Bobby Dazzler to an Iranian man named Saied at the lunch he had planned on October 20, 2007. October 20th is the also the first day that Bobby Dazzler happened to open for business in "M" Mall 17 years ago. Saied arrived 10 minutes late and ordered soup as he wasn't feeling that great. Saied sat next me and Bobby Dazzler faced everybody. He exchanged some nice pleasantries, and some nice talk with the guests took place. The food was great too. It was unusual to be the only woman at the table with five businessmen. It felt a little awkward at first but things got rolling with the great conversation. The rest of us had really great meals with steak or lamb. It was a beautiful day to be out and about. The conversation around the lunch table was very general. How many kids each of us had? How long have we been doing what we have been doing? Where were we born? At the end of lunch, Saied exchanged business cards with Bobby Dazzler and even provided his cellular for contact. He said he would like to get together again sometime. This must have been the individual that Piotr was talking about when he said that he borrowed some money from this Iranian, "Boss". But I had legal documents that I wanted to share if they still thought there were any monies owing on the renovation project, so it didn't bother me at the time. Saied owned a money-exchange business in downtown Vancouver according to his business card. Okay, that is great but I didn't a have need for money exchanging and this individual had a certain presence that was very familiar. It was almost as if I had seen this person before, maybe in another lifetime. Why did he look like a male version of myself? Awkward and weird!?! When he sat down for lunch, his face had the same as expression mine, and for a moment, he was taken aback also. There was a feeling of knowing this person already. It just gnawed away for the whole lunch.

After lunch everyone parted but Saied asked if I could give him a ride back to his business as he had walked over. Sure, no problem! Bobby Dazzler had some more small talk with him but he was told that somehow it felt like I knew him from somewhere. Again, up close, he looked even more like the male version of the self. Weird! As we approached his business, he said "that little, little wee place over there is my small business." He didn't have the demeanor of owning a little currency exchange. Just the way he was dressed made it seem there was much a larger presence that was hard to miss, especially with the sharp suit that he was wearing, the way he spoke with barely any movement to the lips. Kind of like the way the mod leaders in gangster movies like *Godfather* and *Scarface* did. Maybe it was too much movie-watching but this guy had something on his mind. After all, Scott did say that "someone wants to meet you." It had to be this guy. After dropping him off, he said that he would text me soon and asked for my cellular after that. I didn't think that he would actually text anyway.

That soon was a week or so after. Saied asked to have tea at my place since he also lived on the North Shore. Basically, he was inviting himself over. There didn't seem to be any harm in that so he came over in mid-November, 2007. Upon entering the house, he said, "it still looks like you need to do a lot of work in this renovation project." Wait a minute, Piotr is still in negotiation over the house and he still wanted more money. It had been over two years since the legal wrangle started over just how much. Saied was sent by Piotr to see if any additional renovations were done to the home. No renovations would take place as the home was still part of a settlement issue, so it wouldn't have been wise to do any renovations. Bobby Dazzler would end up paying more to Piotr. This guy was just a buddy of Piotr's. He was just coming to check in and that is why Scott said that there was somebody who wants to meet you. I didn't bother discussing any legal wrangling that was going on with Piotr but decided that he can do all the talking.

After tea, Saied said that he wanted to show me some homes that he was working on and asked if I wanted to go for a drive. We drove around the British Properties and other areas as he pointed out several different homes, each time asking if the home should be a renovation or a demolition. Each time the correct answer was given and he seemed surprised. He asked how I knew so much about renos. Bobby Dazzler explained that I had done all the retail-store renovations as a general contactor plus had done many house renovations in the past with my ex-hubby who was a contractor. Basically, I would finance the homes and he would renovate so we could flip them.

Saied sent texts once every two weeks or so. He wanted to just have tea and eventually he became kind of a friend with benefits. After going to his house on the North Shore, it didn't appear that he was a "Boss" from the way he lived. The house he lived in was a dilapidated home that quite possibly was the ugliest home Bobby Dazzler had seen on the North Shore. This man was clearly a "miser" who may be living in misery which included this house. Yuck! The fridge was empty; maybe he ate out all the time. There was very little furniture and it didn't even appear anybody lived in the house. There were positives about him as he introduced me to hot yoga and even invited me to a retreat to see a Master by the name of Dhyan Vimal, which ended up being an amazing experience. Saied continued to see Bobby Dazzler on and off until 2009 when a confrontation took place.

At this time the lawsuit was still going on and was set to go to trial in November 2009. I wanted to see if a settlement was possible. Saied was told that due to a phone call Piotr made to me that he was responsible for getting me thrown out of "M" Mall. He was also told that Piotr was paid all his monies and that I didn't owe him or Piotr any monies. I said that I was aware that Piotr is one of your associates and he took responsibility for having me thrown out of "M" Mall. I want a settlement, NOW!. Piotr had further indicated that he worked for Saied and that he was the "Big Boss" of the Mob. I didn't know if I should have confronted him but the lawsuit was going to summary trial. But this was a way to see what was going on. After attempting to discuss the situation with Saied, he took off like he had seen a ghost. His face become totally white. I asked if I would see him again, he just nodded but ran off and drove 100km per hour down the driveway. Well, that confirmed everything Piotr was saying was true. Subsequent phone calls and emails went unanswered. My hunch was correct!

Piotr called from Poland due to the fact that he had left Canada, after confessing he had Bobby Dazzler thrown out of "M" Mall and did it due to the whole house renovation project going sideways as a way of or revenge. He said that he was in deep trouble with his boss who happened to a be an Iranian by the name of Saied. That is why he had to leave. Piotr indicated that he was working for Saied at the time and that Saied was on the hook for that lawsuit. Just as expected, Saied was indeed the "big boss" according to Piotr. He said that the landlord at "M" Mall was giving Saied problems for what Piotr had done. After asking if a settlement would be coming, Piotr indicated that he, Saied, would rather "smash" Bobby Dazzler and Piotr than ever pay a cent. Nothing was said to Saied about the phone call Piotr had made until that confrontation. The word smash would become important later and was discussed separately.

Since Piotr had been in touch with Bobby Dazzler, all the information was passed along to Sgt. Colin of CFSEU (Combined Forces Special Enforcement Unit), including updates on Saied. Piotr indicated that Bobby Dazzler should seek a settlement with CFSEU. Why would he say that? The only emails received back from Colin were emails that read "thank you for the update". Obviously, serious issues were upon Bobby Dazzler due to the previous house reno business done with Piotr.

As the summer of 2009 passed, the time was coming closer to the Summary Trial and for the possibility of a settlement. Why hadn't Saied bothered to come up with a settlement or discussed the matter with Bobby Dazzler? Was it true that he did NOT want to take responsibility for all the damage that he and Piotr had done at "M" Mall? Was Saied a frenemy? Or just an enemy? Instead of answering the questions, Saied ran out of the house scared like a white ghost. He was sent texts and emails about a settlement but never responded. The last email that Saied was sent went unanswered until a strange email in 2015 arrived from some unknown email address saying that the Bobby Dazzler business was going to be "smashed".

After calling the local police, a File # was obtained in 2015. The police were told that this email may have come from Saied. It appeared that Piotr was not lying in that Saied did not want to take responsibility for what took place at "M" Mall. The summary trial took place in November 2009 with a settlement offer of $5,000. This was refused as that was not the damage that was caused to our business. The wound was much deeper than that now, especially since Bobby Dazzler was able to find out who the individual was that did this to our business and the fact the person who could have helped by offering a proper settlement would rather run off like a girl than man up and pay up. Again, all of this was reported to Sgt. Colin, who simply emailed back saying that maybe Saied was interested in your business and to possibly look at some business brokers. Saied did mention a business broker in passing. That broker's exact name can't be given due to privacy, but the Bobby Dazzler business did in fact go through an evaluation. We will call BS Business Brokers Ltd. which the perfect acronym for them in the manner they evaluated the business. The evaluation came back so low due to no fault of our own we thought it was unfair. We pointed this out and the broker emailed asking how much we felt the business was worth. We gave the exact figure that we wanted as the settlement amount for the lawsuit that was underway. We were told to try to focus on increasing the sales and get back to then. It was not a fair price, given that we been put through extreme problems by Piotr and Saied who were actually linked to this business brokerage firm. When an email was sent to the broker that we are NOT able to sell the business for the price that the broker gave and asked for a much higher price, the very next day a couple of dead bird throws arrived at the house. We even sent a letter to the brokerage firm stating that this firm belongs to Saied and we were aware of it. No response was received. These were reported to Sgt. Colin but no response was ever received. No investigation took place and nobody came to take a report. Obviously, Piotr and Saied plus the business brokerage firm were connected along with Sgt. Colin. It all started to make sense.

All Bobby Dazzler could do was continue doing business normally after the lawsuit was dismissed in late November 2009 plus write the details of our retail ordeal in this "reveal all". Bobby Dazzler thought that problems would cease since the lawsuit was dismissed without a settlement. However, from 2009 to 2017 the retail jail just become more cruel due to this particular connection to Saied.

Focus

So after not listing the retail business for sale in 2009 upon getting a very poor evaluation of it, Bobby Dazzler decided to just focus on sales, growth and improving the profitability of the business. More innovative products and unique items were brought in so that the business could grow and make more money quickly. An independent retailer like Bobby Dazzler is able to quickly change with trends due to it being a smaller retailer. It can shift into the "hot" products with very little effort. Sales, profits and money grew once again. In fact, the profitability of the store was similar to "M" Mall again by 2011, which was a very short time period given the store had only been in the mall for about three-four years. We reported our sales to the landlord as that is part of the lease agreement. However, this time we had more experience dealing with landlords and knew that they obviously were aware when we doing well. Fanny, who was the GM of the mall, even commented on just how far we had come along from the ashes of 2007.

Sales continued on their upswing until Klein walked into our store from BS Business Brokers Ltd. We didn't call this dude and yet, you got it, he shows up! That same broker that was giving us that BS evaluation comes in claiming he had an interested buyer for us. Wanting the store to expand and grow was the best thing for the business, so we actually listed the business this time since sales were on an upswing. The BS brokerage firm is a major firm. It should be pointed out that Klein came in without our contacting him and during one of the best years that Bobby Dazzler was having at "C" Center. ("C" Center is just a name used in place of the actual mall name for privacy reasons.) We started to connect the dots once again by wondering if there was a connection to our reporting great sales to the mall and suddenly this business broker comes waltzing in looking for us to list. After going through all the documents, the business was eventually listed in May 2013 on a one-year contract. We had the business re-evaluated and agreed on a much higher price. Bobby Dazzler had reason to believe that this broker had a buyer already as they were the ones that approached us. We didn't think it would take long to sell given the great numbers that were being produced. Plus, we wanted to move forward from what had happened previously with them for the benefit of the store. What happened after listing was actually the exact opposite of what we thought was going to happen. It appeared these people were just thugs, yes, thugs who wanted to bully our business a little more as if they hadn't done enough.

BULLY

How do you bully a small retailer? And why? Well, firstly we are in the weaker position since we are just a small, independent retailer, owned by a woman. It would be easy to bully a woman and her business around. After listing the business for sale in May 2013, a strange thing happened at home. The home had a small suite that was listed for rent in the summer of 2013. In September, Marcy applied to rent the suite for a year with a lease. After going through the regular process of checking references, she was allowed to move into the suite of the home that was part of the whole fiasco with Piotr. Marcy appeared normal at first, paying her deposit and first month in cash. After that she requested to pay monthly via post-dated cheques. This appeared to be fine until the cheques started to arrive. The cheques were coming from an Iranian by the name of Masoud Salem Khali. Upon asking her why the cheques were not hers, she indicated that her uncle paid her rent. WTF?! This is creepy and weird as she was Caucasian. Here we go again with the Iranians! At that point, since Marcy had not breached any part of the lease agreement, we could not just break her lease and evict her. We simply accepted the form of payment since the cheques cashed each month and payment of the rent was done on a monthly basis. Bobby Dazzler didn't have any real connections/friends who were Iranian but it was hard not to make some sort of connection due to the problems that had taken place with Saied. This was kept in the back of the mind for NOW and written down for this "reveal all", of course.

As preparation for Halloween and Christmas started to happen, Bobby Dazzler made more trips to the United States to clear shipments for the store. It was cheaper, easier and less costly to do all the customs paper work by ourselves than use a broker to do the clearances as they are very expensive. All of a sudden, the Bobby Dazzler SUV was getting inspected each time we crossed into the United States by US CBP (Customs Border Patrol). What was going on here? This secondary inspection would take an extra two to four hours of time since an examination of the vehicle would occur each and every week. This continued right into November and December of that year since many trips were required weekly for inventory to be replenished. Our truck was targeted each and every time. Then in December 2013, Bobby Dazzler had their NEXUS card revoked and taken away without any explanation. A Nexus card is a card that allows the trusted traveler to use the Fast Lane which is faster than the regular line up that takes even longer to cross into the US. After going to an officer who knew me, as I had crossed this border for 23 years without a problem, he said that you didn't hear it from me but it appeared someone was calling me in. He asked if I had a revengeful ex or an ex husband. However, my ex-hubby couldn't have known when I was coming down. Then it started to make sense, the tenant. The only person had to be Marcy since I left the house at 6:30am to go to the States. He further indicated that this person knew each and every time you were coming here. Somebody was giving me business problems for sure. Is there a GPS attached to my truck or what? It had to be the Iranians.

By mid-December 2013, Klein from BS Business Brokers Ltd. came in wondering if we would like to lower the price of the business again. After asking him what happened to the potential buyer of the business, he indicated that they backed out due to some technicality. It didn't appear coincidental that Klein dropped by asking to lower the price for some strange reason. He said that the business had been on the market for seven months and that maybe a drop was necessary. He said maybe it is time for you to get out while you can. What is that supposed to mean? We didn't believe that a drop was necessary. The problems at the border continued as now Canada Customs started to give us problems when we crossed back into Canada with our shipments. Our deliveries, packages and boxes were all being opened and inspected every single time. Going to the United States to pick up our parcels was no longer as cost-effective. In fact, the time that was being taken at the border was time that could have been spent in the store selling

In January 2014, we voiced our choice not to lower the price of the business any further. Klein was disappointed and said that we would change our minds in a few months. In the meantime, we hadn't seen any mail come for our tenant since October 2013. After getting suspicious of her and her reasons for living downstairs, this made us write back to Sgt. Colin that there might be tenant who is connected to Piotr and Saied living downstairs that is causing us problems at the US and Canada borders when we cross. That email was sent in April

2014. Plus, we voiced concerns that her cheques were coming from an Iranian by the name of Masoud Khalili. We were just putting two and two together.

Within one day of sending that email, Marcy came upstairs giving Bobby Dazzler her notice to terminate the lease due to her desire to relocate to Gibsons. Well, that was a another coincidence. Bobby Dazzler told the cops that the tenant downstairs might be a fake tenant planted there due to issues that kept coming up at the border and then the tenant wants to move the very next day after letting CFSEU know that she is a fake. WTF? The response was, it was just a "coincidence".

Well, this just got a little juicier! In May 2014, the contract for the business listing was going to lapse and we decided to pull the plug and not bother with the listing any longer since we were sure that business interference, racketeering, business problems and issues were all connected back to BS Business Brokers, Saied, Piotr and now Sgt. Colin. These characters were all on the same team! They not only wanted to bully Bobby Dazzler at work but also successfully got a fake tenant to live in my house while the business was listed, in order to further their business-bullying by racketeering the business further.

After sending BS Business Brokers Ltd. a final email, stating that they may shred the documents that were provided for the business, they asked if I wanted to further extend the contract to sell the business. We had had enough already of these bullies and decided that we would simply tell the story to others, to reveal what truly happened to the successful local retailers who were bullied constantly. The constant bullying increased daily upon lapse of the contract with numerous resumes coming in from only Iranians. We weren't hiring so the sudden influx of resumes was noted by our Store Manager who said that it was weird that only one group was applying for jobs at our store when we don't even have a posting. We knew exactly who these resumes were connected to - Saied.

Rival

It wasn't enough that Bobby Dazzler was being bullied in the retail store daily but we had more to rival with by 2013. Despite their being verbal agreements with the mall that our competitors would not be enticed to come to our complex, we had to face the music when they all started to arrive. In the retail world, the rival is the main competitor of a retail store. Usually, a retailer likes to sign a lease in a mall that doesn't have any competitors. That would be the ideal situation. Our mall had only 180 stores and the rival was actually coming in to compete with us. But by late 2013, our main competitor, Spencer's Gifts, had arrived and plus a temp store called Mind Games was added to take all the cream off of the top of all the great sales that we had been enjoying for the past few years. It took a couple of years for Spencer's to actually hit our business, as many people didn't even know they were at the hidden location. This made it very difficult to continue retailing with the same passion as in the past. It simply meant that we were going to be going back to the same cycle that Bobby Dazzler experienced at "M" Mall when this rival came and left after retailing for only about five years. Thus, the rival just seemed to accentuate the already frustrating situation of dealing with the bully.

The rival is always an issue, no matter which business one gets into. However, the rival can also be a competitor that actually works for a specific retailer and then takes the idea, the supplier names, even some of the staff and decides to open shop right inside the same mall as the original retailer. Thus, the rival can very well be a staff member that decides that the business idea is so good that they might as well take the idea for themselves. Thus, there are actually two types of rivals in the retail world of inline stores.

In 1990 when Bobby Dazzler opened, there was no rival to the business. The closest at the time would have been Sharper Image. However, this chain was based out of the United States and there were no locations in Canada. Bobby Dazzler seemed to have cornered the market when it came to gizmos, gadgets and gifts up until about 2003 when things really started to get shaken up. That is when Spencer's Gifts opened shop in "M" Mall and when Bobby Dazzler saw its sales plummet. The rival Spencer's Gifts put a real dent into our sales momentum or lack thereof after they arrived. Competitors definitely make a big difference when they are around.

This was not the end of it either for Bobby Dazzler. In early 2000, an employee by the name of Roger was hired who claimed that Bobby Dazzler was his most favorite store in the whole world. Of course, he excelled in sales and did well. However, right after the "M" Mall completed its redevelopment, expansion and renovation, Roger left our store to set up shop in the exact same mall we were in. He had taken all the supplier names, addresses, phone numbers and even some of the staff to open a competing business called Gizmos. This meant that there were rivals who came from the United States competing with us now but also a rival that were trained, paid and previously employed by us who decided to hijack the idea for themselves.

By, 2007 just after having the most amazing 2006 in sales, the landlord decided not to renew our lease after operating for 17 years in the complex. This particular problem shined light on the fact that without a lease, there is no retail business. The lease is obviously the most important part of the retail business unless one owns the building themselves. This is examined in detail in *Lease* and in *Shawn*.

So, after going through a horrible experience at "M" Mall due to the non-renewal of our lease, Bobby Dazzler decided to head over to a mall that didn't have any rivals. Bobby Dazzler chose a mall 30 minutes out in the suburbs called "C" Mall. After several meetings with the landlord and picking an ideal location, Bobby Dazzler was reassured that none of the rivals were being lured into the mall. Bobby Dazzler was given their word verbally that no competitors would be brought in. This was very important to our retail store since we were spending a significant amount on leasehold improvement/ interests. That amount was well over $100K. For a small retailer that is significant. Plus, Bobby Dazzler signed up for a 10-year lease which is a significant commitment. After humming along for five years, Bobby Dazzler was shocked to find out that Spencer's Gifts was opening up in the mall. After approaching the landlord about the issue, Bobby Dazzler was told to change up their products to be more competitive. "You can do it"! It appeared that the landlord did not keep their word. Naturally, Bobby Dazzler felt betrayed. Sales plummeted after the second year of their opening in a small suburban mall that we were located in. It appeared that the landlord did not care about loyalty and thought that it would be fine to share our sales with Spencer's Gifts who was our direct rival. That's when we started to wonder why did we ever agree to come in this mall? It felt like fraud in our eyes.

To add insult to injury, the landlord signed up two-three temps during peak seasonal periods of Halloween and Christmas to make sure that whatever profits that were left over would have to be split up even more so that NO profits were left to us to make. Is there a point to continue retailing? Who are the temps? Well, temps became the third rival that will be discussed separately later. It became clear that the retailer does not have control over their own business even if they try their best. The rival seems to be lurking on the outside and on the inside of all retail businesses. This applies to all businesses but retailers seem to face this problem even more so today.

The best way to counter the rival that might be working inside the store is to have all employees sign confidentiality agreements. These agreements protect the business from the likes of Roger or other employees who would like to become competitors, and work in a business solely to obtain trade secrets. This agreement can be found online or one can be drafted by a lawyer that is suited to the needs of one's own retail business or any business.

As for outside competitors, they will always be there and it is difficult to get a landlord to agree to a non-compete. However, a reputable landlord would be one who has fair dealings. This was found to be very difficult in our experience with the many "large" landlords who simply acted heavy-handed on many levels with the small retailer. The only way to fix this problem was to revise business practices through proper business ethics. They will be discussed later in *Ethic*. The modern-day rival for the bricks and mortar store was no longer just a competitor in the mall. It was cyberspace and online that was something that could no longer be controlled, no matter what. The small retailer could never compete with "endless aisles" online.

PESTS

Nobody likes pests! There were many different kinds of pests that approached Bobby Dazzler. Pests were primarily interested in obtaining consent. This was done attempted by through the following different ways:

- Phone calls
- Email
- Physically approaching the business and attempting to get consent by visiting the retail store

Initially, the pests would call and harass us with those annoying phone calls wondering if we wanted another credit card. After dealing with the constant bullying, Bobby Dazzler went on to deal with pests. Who were the pests in the retail world? After pulling the plug on the business listing with BS Business Brokers Ltd., the personal and business bullying led to numerous annoying calls from pests. The calls started in mid-2014 on a daily, weekly, monthly and yearly basis. The calls arrived from credit card companies wondering if we needed another American Express, a Visa or another Mastercard. The only catch was they would ask for the owner of the business by name each and every time. These pests were clearly targeting Bobby Dazzler and were not just trying to reach 'just' anybody. Why anybody would agree to get a credit card over the phone via a telemarketer is just mind-boggling. Naturally, we never agreed to get another credit card from these annoying calls.

After declining the credit cards offers, the calls moved over to loans. These calls started to come from companies wondering if they could speak to the owner of the business to see if we need a business loan or a personal loan. Both of which require the company to pull a credit report. These type of calls were rare prior to 2014. However, once the plug was pulled from BS Business Brokers Ltd., the calls were sometimes excess.

The next manner the pests attempted to obtain the consent of Bobby Dazzler was through email communications. Our email box was full of requests to see if we wanted some more monies for inventory or if we wanted an advance on our credit card payments. Once again in each of these cases, a credit report would need to be pulled. Knowing that it is never very wise to engage with a business or a person who approaches us, we declined all email requests by deleting all the emails.

When the email requests were declined, the mailbox started to get full. Mail started to arrive weekly whereby a pre-approved loan in the form of a check was made out to the owner of Bobby Dazzler. All the owner had to do was deposit the check to use the funds, immediately. Alas, there was fine print on the back of the check that read, "upon deposit the loan company would be able to pull a credit report on the individual business owner." It was not only obvious but apparent that someone was targeting us, particularly the owner of the business, to get a credit report. It is very, very important not to let anybody pull a credit report, especially if it is not necessary for any business or person. This is just common sense.

When the above three methods of obtaining a credit report or consent failed, other avenues were attempted. Suddenly, the supervisor for Canada Post Commercial/Small Business happened to come into the store to see if we wanted to open up a small business or commercial account with them for mailing out merchandise. The supervisor dropped by twice in one month and drove all the way from Richmond which is an hour's drive to get to our store. We were not interested but it should be pointed out that in order to open a Commercial Account with Canada Post, a credit report would need to get pulled, plus on the agreement in very fine print, Canada Post would be given consent to access the business' bank accounts at the various financial institutions that the business conducts its transactions with from time to time. Time to time can be understood as anytime or all the time. Why would anybody agree to this? This seems quite broad and an overreaching privacy law but many individuals actually don't understand until one reads what that they are signing away. Bobby Dazzler was paying close attention by now to ALL the different pests that would arrive. They were carefully documented as the Canada Post supervisor left his business card twice along with an application for a Commercial Account each time. Since this guy had drive an hour to get to us, he was insistent! We didn't bother getting back to him since we were NOT interested and didn't do that many mailings. The annoying calls, emails and mail continued.

Nevertheless, the calls got so annoying that Bobby Dazzler got an answering machine. Nobody left messages, they actually wanted to speak to someone. A quick Google search revealed that the numbers belonged to third-party credit/debit processors who wanted to find out if we wanted to lower the rates of our Visa/Mastercard processing fees and lower the rates for the monthly rate of rental for the terminal used to process these transactions. The catch in each and every case that a credit report with consent needed to pulled. We were definitely not interested in changing our Merchant processor as Bobby Dazzler had used the same company since inception in 1990. Suddenly, the supervisor from our own credit card processor showed up and asked if wanted to join the gift card program. The only catch was to sign the bottom of the form and agree to consent to a credit report. Hey, wait a minute! Why would we need to consent to a credit report when Bobby Dazzler is a corporation and not a proprietorship. Also, if we are already doing business with this company since 1990, then there is no need to consent to a credit report. These calls came daily by this time. After asking one of the providers, what is involved in getting a quote, they all indicated that they would need to pull a credit report to even give a quote. Well, that was no surprise at all. Why would you need to do that for just a quote is beyond any reasonable understanding.

In July 2016, a company called CPC Credit Processing Canada popped in to see the owner of the business. Having gone through so much harassment, we didn't trust any business approaching our business. This company had a business card with the Canadian flag on it. They indicated that they wanted to make sure we were receiving the right rate for our Visa/Mastercard/American Express when processing transactions. We took the business card. A quick Google search revealed a website that was NOT operating. The individual that owned the website was an individual by the name of Lucky. The address on the card was the address of "M" Mall without a unit number. Weird! His company was a cloud company. An online company search revealed that no such private/partnership/corporation existed but a further NUANS search is much more in-depth and includes federal and private companies, and revealed that this company was a federally registered company of Canada. It was in partnership with Lucky. Wait a second! CPC Credit Processing Canada sounds really familiar; that was on some document that left was left at the store. Oh yes! How could we forget, CPC Credit Processing Canada stands for Canada Post Corporation Credit Processing. It is simply an acronym. Just speculating, right?!? So, in failing to convince Bobby Dazzler to open up a Commercial Account with Canada Post, this scam artist was trying to use deception to convince us that we need to analyze our VISA/Mastercard rates with them. This is fraud and a scam! The only problem was that it was a company in partnership with Lucky. Saied was behind this for sure. He was causing these pests to come in over and over again, his contacts. By now, Bobby Dazzler was spending more time taking annoying calls, visits, reading nonsense emails and opening mail from those that wanted to loan us money, give us another credit card or wanted us to open up some sort of account that required a credit report to be pulled than sales/selling. Some of the emails came from well-known places that all people deal with like Rogers, Shaw, Paypal, Equifax, Twitter and Facebook asking for a quick "click" for consent to their new updated privacy agreement. They claimed to want permission to continue to send emails to us by clicking the "I consent" box. But, who knows what someone was consenting to? Other emails required us to click on a link to verify an account, to update a password or simply requesting us to click somewhere inside the email. The best thing to do was to delete all emails that arrive for any business person and NEVER agree to any companies' privacy agreement. Why? The large do business with the large. This is deception and very deceptive business practices to say the least. The focus from being a retailer was definitely shifting to just wondering what is going to be next. We were getting really tired by now and started to feel as if retail was just indeed a jail.

Worse

Could things actually get any worse for our retail world? Apparently, yes! 2016 turned out to be the worst year in sales for the "C" Center location. Our anchoring neighbor West49 pulled out of the mall. The clients that shopped in this store were our clientele. After, they left their vacated store sat empty for six months before an Asian bakery and Asian bank was put in mid-2016. These two retailers did not help sales at all as they didn't have our clientele. Now, the lease was completely too expensive due to NO traffic coming by and extra noise that was being created by the demolition and construction crews for the new stores that were due to arrive in six months to eight months time from our anchor tenant West49 leaving.

Bobby Dazzler had no choice but asked for rental abatement and that is when we got a Lease Amending Agreement (LAA). However, the rental abatement included came with a new clause added in illegally. This document had clause 15.26 added in which was a Privacy Clause. Our original lease document ended at clause 15.25. The Privacy Clause was meant to be signed by proprietors and partnerships only. The landlord attempted to force us to sign this document by stating that that was the only way that they would abate or provide rental relief. This was illegal. After signing, the document was returned to our store with a demand that we sign the new clause. WE REFUSED and produced the landlord's own blank form of the lease document. It clearly stated that the Privacy Clause was not supposed to be signed by a Corporation which is what our retail store was and had signed the lease as. The Privacy Clause was yet another attempt to pull a personal credit report on the owner of Bobby Dazzler. There was no need to do that since we had been at the center for nine years and already had a lease. We were already doing business with the landlord. This was the heavy-handed approach that Bobby Dazzler had to deal with when it came to the ethics of the large landlord dealings.

Our lease was up next year and the prospect of renewing in this location looked dismal. Even moving to another location inside the same mall was not going to cut it as it meant spending another 100-150K for renovations, higher rent for a better location and still having to deal with those pests that didn't want to stop bullying us. The Winter of 2016 came and it was the worst Christmas selling season that Bobby Dazzler had in "C" Center due to the amount of snow and ice that came. The rooftop parking was closed on December 2 which is probably the worst time to close off 800 spots for parking. It didn't reopen till December 23. The damage was already done! Bobby Dazzler ordered and sales plummeted 35%. This was not good!

It didn't help having the US exchange hover around 37%. It was so difficult to order stuff for a profit at this point. The surprise win by Trump in the US election further threw people off due to uncertainty. It was like pulling teeth to get people who actually made it out of the snow to the mall to spend money. The transit authority excitedly opened up the rapid transit line in December also in hopes that more people would come to the mall. However, all that did was have people leave this mall that had 170 stores and go to our old mall, "M" Mall via a 30-minute transit ride and enjoy 550 stores for more selection and variety. This turned out to be a shot in the foot for "C" Center. Looking at all the shops that closed in 2016, the dismal sales of the Christmas selling season, the horrible US exchange rate, the use of transit to go from our to mall to the bigger "M" mall plus the higher anticipated rents coming with a new lease just put a damper in retailing. It really started to feel like the walls were closing in on this jail. That passion to come to the store was gone. With so many factors causing this feeling of being burned out and wiped out, Bobby Dazzler felt retail was futile.

After asking management for a snow-removal contract and none being available for the tenants (who actually paid into it) due to the landlord's Privacy in this case, we asked that we receive rental abatement again. It was not fair to pay $10,000.00 and not have the snow shoveled. The landlord must not have had a contract as the rooftop stayed closed during the most crucial selling times of December 2-December 21, 2017. Just relying on global warming and hoping for the best could not have been the business plan. It certainly would have saved the landlord a ton of money not having any type of contract in place or a proper plan. As a retailer who is on the hook for $10,000 + a month for rent, that is just not good enough. Poor mall management should not be the responsibility of the retailer. This problem was a big one and it wasn't one that Bobby Dazzler was willing to take a chance with in the winter of 2018. Our lease was coming up and we were weary of all the issues that retail had brought to us. By January 2017, the business started to deplete personal savings. Could things get any worse than the 2016 year?

AUDIT

After experiencing our second worst Christmas selling season with respect to sales and with only six months to go on our lease, strange calls started to arrive from 604-951-5660 on Friday, January 6th. The call display read that it was the Government of Canada calling, not Canada Revenue Agency (CRA). Smelled like a spoofing scam! A quick Google search revealed that this number was on the BAD number list. It was even connected to a company called BS Resource Services which was apparently a criminal debt collector. WTF is going on! After contacting CRA (Canada Revenue Agency) directly through their 1-800 number, they revealed that they had not called and there was NO audit being initiated by CRA. The CRA officer on the phone was a little hesitant in his voice but said you should call that Sammy guy on the letter and give him what he wants. Just the fact that CRA officer was hesitant on the phone made Bobby Dazzler feel there was something definitely fishy going on here. Having gone through many audits in the past, the audit process was something that Bobby Dazzler knew. This smelled like a scam. Unfortunately, there are many CRA scams out there and we read about them all the time in the newspaper or online. This same number called my business twice and once on my home fax machine which is an unlisted number that CRA does not have. Naturally, the call was left to go to the answering machine. No messages were left, again.

On Tuesday, January 10th, a burly-sounding male voice knocks on the house door claiming to be from the post office. Oh no, not you guys again, I thought. After opening the door and not recognizing the postman, the "so-called" postman said that he had registered mail document for Bobby Dazzler. After living in the same house for 12 years, you get to know the postman and even give him chocolates for Christmas. This guy was NOT the postman. Something in the gut said that this guy is a fraud. He asked me twice to sign for the documents which appeared to be from CRA (Canada Revenue Agency). Instead, I asked that the letters be carded as Bobby Dazzler was not home. He left the Registered Mail card for the Mail to be picked up later at the Post Office. The store called and said that some CRA (Canada Revenue Agency) documents arrived via registered mail to the store.

Well, if staff have already signed for them at the store then there was no need to pick up them personally at the Post Office again. They are the same documents. Plus, it should be pointed out that Bobby Dazzler does not agree to the Terms and Conditions of our national post company. By signing for those documents one is just giving consent or permission to the national post service which a part of the Government of Canada to look through one's personal and business bank accounts. Reading the fine print in business is always a good idea.

The next day, the letters were opened! The letters appeared to be from the CRA but the letterhead was off. The letterhead was photocopied and faint from an original that I had at home. This was a bogus audit. Knowing full well what a real audit was since we had experienced so many in the past from various government organizations, this one was definitely not a real audit. It was just a tactic to get Bobby Dazzler to agree to the Terms and Conditions of the national post company. It should be pointed out that since no proper response ever arrived from the police after numerous complaints made about the shady characters like Piotr, Saied and others, it appears that this "fake" audit came from the police. This confirmed that Piotr and Saied were in fact working with the police. If you want to take the head off a person, the best way is to get all their assets frozen. Yes, this was also seen in all those gangster movies that talk about how the Feds can do this to people. No response from the police since 2005, with the exception of one meeting to give the police all the information that Piotr gave me, resulted in this. After calling my cousin who was a Chartered Accountant, he said it sounded like a lifestyle investigation or audit but he would have see the documents personally to confirm. CRA (Canada Revenue Agency) can do this but the individual must give consent to the Terms and Conditions of the national post company. Well, Bobby Dazzler already knew this and wasn't going to be signing any documents nor giving consent.

No response was given to the letters. However, Sammy walked in on January 20 wondering when he could start the audit. He brought the same letters into the store that were sent to the store via Registered Mail. I told him that I thought he was bogus to his face. He presented a business card which appeared to be Canada Revenue Agency but it was freshly perforated. After he left, we again called our second-cousin, an accountant, who was a partner at a major firm and expressed our concerns. He said that this sounded more like an investigation not an audit, which are 2 totally different things according to him and online searches. Audits are done by CRA but investigations are done by police.

Well, that puts two and two together. This can also be Googled if one is interested. Retailers and all business people should know what the difference is. To put it into easy terms, an audit is a compliance check which requires the taxpayer to comply. An investigation is usually criminal and does not require the tax payer to produce anything, since the punishment can be jail time and/or harsher than an audit. There is no need to comply. He said that someone may have called you out due to gossip or just trying to give you financial trouble or problems. After explaining to him that many calls had been coming in from pests who were trying to obtain a credit report on me in the past, he said that someone is being vindictive, disruptive and wants to give you financial problems. It should be pointed out that after making complaints against Saied in 2015, the police never got back to me. Perhaps, this guy did in fact have the police "in his back pocket" as he indicated and as Piotr had said. Or, perhaps Saied is a government informant or an agent of some sort who was abusing his power to cause financial problems for our business and myself. It appeared online that he was still running around town and not in arrested for stalking or criminal harassment due to the complaints that I had made against him.

Then it dawned on Bobby Dazzler that the documents had a middle name put in them that is only used on my driver's license but not used with CRA. Cops have access to drivers' licenses. Ah haa! Instead of getting back to me, the cops just decided to get back at me. This was starting to make more sense! Well, if consent is given to look at the bank accounts, that could cause a lot of problems. In fact, it could cause one to have their personal/business accounts frozen or have this Saied guy walk in and attempt to take the business over for free since the accounts are frozen due to his working in concert or "contacts" with the government. This Saied started to sound like an embezzler or an extortionist of some sort. Why bother calling the cops if you're just going to have problems, right?

Bobby Dazzler did not get back to Sammy, the CPA/CGA acting on behalf of CRA. He showed up again on February 8 asking if we were ready for the audit. Bobby Dazzler wanted to see what this man was going to do with the books and records. They are kept in the store stockroom all the time. There was already a chair and desk there. My assistant manager and I just wanted to watch him and his partner. So, instead of going through the documents, Sammy pulled out a scanner, only scanned all the bank statements but did not do any auditing. He scanned for a bit. After that time, he indicated that there were some statements missing, the numbers didn't match up and he thinks that there might be some tax evasion. Right?!? He made this statement due to some missing statements. Those statements were missing on purpose as they were taken out just to see what going on with this so-called audit by Sammy. Actually, many statements were missing. At this point, there were statements in the scanner that weren't even mine or belonging to my business. Tax evasion is an investigation not an audit. Now he demanded three years of bank statements and credit-card receipts. Bobby Dazzler told him everything would be ready in three weeks. We had no plans on giving this guy a thing.

In the meantime, we mailed him a Cease and Desist letter. When he arrived at the end of February, he was presented the Cease and Desist letter and tried to give it back to us. After working in the CRA's mail room in 1987/1988, Bobby Dazzler was aware that all letters sent to CRA are kept on file. Letters are not given back to tax-payers that send them in to CRA. This was definitely some sort of shakedown. After going into deep thought, a judgment call had to be made. This was a phony audit. Sammy was given the letter again and told never to show up again. We didn't cooperate with him and his so-called audit. We didn't answer any of his calls, either, as the call display showed the number calling.

From March 2017 to May 2017, other compliance issues suddenly came about. This just meant that CRA was essentially bouncing between a lifestyle audit, investigation audit and a compliance audit which is all illegal of course and very heavy handed. Well, that wasn't surprising since these were the same type of things that had experienced at "M" Mall, already. Fraser Health came into the store on three occasions, claiming that our store was selling vaporizers to kids age 14 or 15 years old. However, no receipt was ever produced for these allegations. This was false information. There were six other retailers in the mall that sold vaporizers. Naturally, we voiced our concerns that it was not a real complaint. Bobby Dazzler asked to see who complained. Citing privacy reasons, we were unable to determine who even filed the complaint. Our store did not sell any vaporizers to any underage children. Our store just got a warning notice for this alleged non-compliance issue. We were further told to cover up the smoke case with black paper so that kids and actually nobody could see what was inside of it without producing proper ID. This caused the sales of the top-selling items to plummet. If the case is blacked out then NO sales came from this case, which actually paid the rent from January to September as previously mentioned. This would be fine but right across from us was a newsstand retailer that sold tobacco products along with all the products that we sold. Bobby Dazzler asked why they were not required to cover up the showcases with black as they were selling the exact same items as we were. Additionally, they have more minors coming in to purchase pop, ice cream and chips so they have a higher number of minors coming into the store than we did. The officer said that she would find time to visit that retailer soon.

Next, the fire department, which normally came every August, shows up in mid-May. They indicated that they were looking for the fire door. We don't have a fire door. If these guys were really from the fire department then they already know we don't have a fire door for this unit. We just have one front door to the store. Normally, a retail store blocks the fire door with stock/inventory, this can cause a non-compliance complaint to be written up by the fire department which is related to the whole bogus audit. These were fake fire department guys, they looked dumbfounded when we told them that there was NO fire door. Well, now we suspected that the CFSEU (police) was behind this. If we had a door and it had been blocked, the fire department would write us up for not-complying. This non-compliance report would then be used by CFSEU to get an order from a judge to claim we were evading taxes based on this non-compliance order. That is the way this works! The fire department was just looking for a reason to write us up so that we could be given notice for non-compliance which could very well cause the so called "tax evasion" investigation to continue so that some financial problems for Bobby Dazzler can occur. This fire-door inspection was triggered and connected to the CFSEU complaint about Saied and everything else related to compliance at all levels of government.

Sammy tried to call the store once in the third week of May 2017 but we never returned his call. In the meantime, we had strange calls from our own friends asking tax related questions. My best buddy, Hassan, asked if he could put the transmission bill that he recently got for his daughter in his taxes. Debby called to see if she could come over. Once over, she asked monetary questions about the house renovations. This was someone who never spoke about money. Weird?!? Betsy texted to see if I wanted to attend a black-tie event for which the tickets are $1,000+ That is really expensive, no thank you. Strange of her to ask but it was all connected to this bogus audit. I guess police were listening to my phone and ringing up friends to see if anybody would be able to turn on me. Were friends or so-called friends were being approached to find out information or to see if non-compliance was taking place? This was harassment at the hands of government/police, malicious persecution and criminal harassment for 14 years to say the least. It seemed like a story similar to what good old uncle Erwin Braich was attempting to provide the public to see. It can be viewed on YouTube by searching "tax fraud" and "Erwin Braich".

He was even looking to find someone to write a story about his for him for $1 million dollars. That is where the idea to write this whistle-blowing, "reveal all" story for business people to see. Others were already telling their inspiring and moving stories on #metoo and #iamresilient via Social links. Erwin Braich was able to create a YouTube about his story. This individual went through quite a of bit financial chaos, abuse and horror just because of a document that he purportedly signed via Registered Mail. Reading stories such as these was very helpful in determining what was going on. Full details were known to Bobby Dazzler prior to going through this experience. That is why Bobby Dazzler knew NEVER, ever to sign any documents that arrive via Registered Mail from anybody.

By the end of May 2017, the police came into the store looking to speak to our part-time sales clerk who sold a $1, penis-shaped lollipop to a 15 -year-old. None of the staff thought anything was wrong with selling that as no ID is required for lollipops. But the "major" crimes division came in the store claiming that a random 45-year-old man gave the 15-year-old the $1.15 and was attempting to lure her by buying her candy. The sales clerk didn't even think the man in the store and the two teenagers were related or together. This resulted in another investigation taking place that occupied the next two weeks. Our store was about to close at the end of the next month. We just had more and more of the same issues week after week. Problems, abusive behavior at the hands of the police and ongoing interference in the store. Bobby Dazzler was literally done with retailing at this point. We were hopeful that once the store closed that we would no longer have to deal with the problems and issues.

All the previous calls and this situation provided more evidence that someone was just being nasty and going around town creating gossip of tax evasion: slander among all the other accusations. But that someone got narrowed down to who when the well-dressed Iranian lady who did nothing came over from the kids' hair salon across from us to ask if she could purchase some sexy, large-sized costumes for herself without paying tax. She asked if we could do the sale without a receipt. Naturally, we said "NO, I would have to give you a receipt". Then an Iranian body laser company came in see if she could sell Bobby Dazzler a $3,000 laser-body contour package. That would be a very expensive package given how much I made. Two weeks after going to get prices for some appliances, a Persian-accented man calls asking if I need any financing for the purchase of my appliances. I just said that I was checking prices. Obviously, I was being followed around. Being fully aware and alert helped in declining all these people approaching us. But Bobby Dazzler always suspected that Saied was behind these people the whole time. He did say that he was going to use his wealth to pay for contacts to "smash" our business.

Narcs, which is short for narcissists, often spend lots of money in order to smash people they are unable to control. This guy was an extortionist, embezzler and thief, just as Piotr had stated, years ago and he was not going to stop at anything until he got the money that Piotr owed him. That meant he wanted to continue in his attempt to smash me, my business and my children. Calls were not made to the police anymore as they were not going to help Bobby Dazzler. They were in on this too. We were provided with two separate File numbers from our local police. One was from 2015 and another was from 2017. It was apparent, and no doubt this bogus audit was brought on by him also. Everything is always connected and it always a good idea to be awake, alert and aware!

Sam never showed up again. At the time of writing no court-ordered documents ever arrived and it had been many months by this time. This was something that was brought on by BS Resource Services. They claimed to be a business services company but it was NOT! Was it a company that was in partnership with the government? I assume if the government wants to take the head off of someone, they send in these guys to do it.

However, in August after about a month and half of being out of the mall, the postman arrived with more Registered Mail documents. My underage daughter signed the documents in her name with NO last name. After going online and to check the signatory name that appeared on the document that was signed, the post office claimed that it was Bobby Dazzler who had signed these documents. This was untrue, false and fraudulent, plus I knew where this was all going. A call was made to the national post office requesting that it be changed to the correct name as the signatory line showed it to be my signature when it was my daughter who signed with just her first name. A service ticket number was issued and the national post company did not call nor write back to this problem. We sent a complaint letter that very day to the national post company via mail and fax. We did not receive any calls back until mid-September when Bobby Dazzler was told that the name could not be changed.

By mid-September, a girlfriend named Sally who had moved to Montreal five years ago wanted to come see me after five years. This was a little strange as we had grown apart by then. She claimed to have no place to stay around the time of my birthday and said that she wanted to come celebrate my birthday and make up lost time between us. So, I agreed and waited till she would arrive in early October. Let's see what she wants.

On September 13, 2017, a proposal letter arrived from Sammy representing CRA asking if they could send me a tax assessment for nearly a million dollars. What? Were they asking my permission to see if that was okay for me? No way! I hadn't signed for any documents via Registered Mail nor had I given consent. This was pointed out to Sammy via regular mail and faxed confirmation. On October 13th, 2017, more documents arrived via Registered Mail that we did not sign. Sammy even sent the same documents via regular mail and he claimed that he didn't get a response to the proposal letter when in fact we had sent a faxed response and letter via regular mail on September 13, 2017. We got our faxed confirmation as proof. These people were liars! This proved that not only was the signature improperly used, a bogus assessment was being attempted by Sammy. This was indeed a scam! Bobby Dazzler had a post-office box at the local pharmacy where some company mail and left-over bills would arrive after winding down the company from the retail operations of the summer. Sammy sent registered mail documents there and left them in the mail box without a signature. Illegally! Good thing my kids work at the pharmacy and noticed, right?!? Usually when Registered Mail documents arrived in the post office box, they are signed by the postman or the pharmacy post office manager. After tracking the document online, it appeared that it was still in transit when it was in my hand. This is illegal. Perhaps an illegal signature was being attempted by Sammy and BS resource services. The letter was taken to the post-office manager and it was sent back as being refused. The post-office manager was told all mail going to this box arrived via Registered Mail could be refused.

By October 2017, Sally had arrived. She looked a lot bigger and not really in the greatest of shape. I guess things fall apart when you age and don't work out. She appeared off, for sure. Her main desire was to going shopping. I wasn't going back to retail even for personal shopping as it disinterested me that much. Something I was not interested in given I was writing this very manuscript at the time and I just left the retail jail. I never told her a thing of what was going on otherwise she may not have come as I would have figured out why she was coming. Every day she asked if we could shopping. She was interested in spending money. Easy for her as she was apparently on disability and had a rich hubby who just wanted her to go shopping. When we did one day in the mall, she attempted to push me into making large purchases of things that I did not need. Purchases such as a scrubbing machine for the face that was over $100 at Sephora. She also didn't pay for any meals so I decided that I was just going to eat at home. Who wants to go to the mall if you're writing about retail and the jail it was. She knew I was writing a book but was too interested in getting drunk on gin and wine that she didn't know I was paying more attention to her behavior and her actions. This frustrated her. Then she wanted to online shop which is something that I don't ever do. I don't trust it! It appeared that Sally was really interested in spending my money. At my own birthday dinner, she didn't even offer to pay so my sister ended up paying for everyone. She started calling my cellular asking about ridiculous online business ventures. I thought by this time that she was stupid and could NOT wait till she left. It was my hope that I never see her again. Clearly, she too was fishing for something and her behavior was abnormal. Maybe she was sent in by the cops to check me out. By the end of her trip, she was told that our friendship was no longer. She was told to lose my number!

On October 13, 2017, a tax assessment based on some bogus numbers arrived that was close to $1,000,000 million dollars. A letter of objection was written immediately to CRA. This process takes 5-7 months to go through but there was no consent given to go into my bank accounts and so many transactions that were not mine were being put into this proposal letter. Obviously, a scam! Normally, if due process is not used the assessment is supposed to be vacated. That is the proper process that CRA is supposed to take. However, that is not the route that was taken with Bobby Dazzler. CRA asked PayPal to produce all the records of the Bobby Dazzler transactions for PayPal. Well, we had abandoned our website more than five years ago. There were no transactions during the past five years. The major lesson for all business, not just ours, was that consent should never, ever be given to third-party processors, with fine print attached for anyone using their services.

Meanwhile, calls and emails still arrived that were phishing emails, looking for us to "click" some part or the email that would have "consent" in it. We deleted all emails. The assessment was supposed to have been vacated back in October 2017, but the crooks attempted to obtain consent even during the objection period which is illegal. Somebody must have some real pull, wealth, or a strong partnership with the CRA to do this for such a long time. This had to be Saied. CRA persisted on getting consent, which was never, ever going to happen. This particular bogus audit along with the ordeal needed to be written about since it owuld help other retail businesses or business owners know that this, too, could happen to them. The tax authority seemed to bounce between a lifestyle audit, investigative audit and compliance audit over the years. Abusing the laws and the system just as Mr. Braich had experienced over his years dealing with similar issues with the large organizations. One does not need to produce any documents once it has been confirmed though intuition or through a judgment call that this might be the case, especially due to past dealings with the police and their non-action or updates. Naturally, it is hard to determine that until the auditor arrives and his actions are observed. As much detail was provided to the reader to assist in any dealings that they may have with CRA. This was essentially the straw that broke Bobby Dazzler's back. Our business had became a literal retail jail in reality in so many ways. After investigating the company, BS contact resources, it was established that it was a business connected to Saied and his family. Everything is always connected even in business. So, complaints made to the police lead to Bobby Dazzler being handed over to the wolf, Saied, himself.

The preceding is meant to assist anybody who may have a business enemy, a ex-partner who may want to give financial problems, a wife/ hubby who want to get back at somebody for doing them wrong or revenge. This is information is for all to know. All business or individuals would find the following really important information in a general terms in dealings with the tax authorities. This was a regular *Godfather* story where authorities are called to take down an enemy or competitor. Well, they were successful in getting rid of this retailers' desire to retail again.

CEASE

By time 2016 finished up, Bobby Dazzler was excited to end our lease. Retail just wasn't what it used to be. We got official notice that another tenant had been found for our spot and if we wanted to leave on June 30 that we could take that opportunity. We accepted the offer from the landlord to leave early and felt as if we got our "Get Out of Jail Free Card". The game would be over for Bobby Dazzler after 27 years, as it was for so many other retailers. This can be seen by goggling retailers, major retailers closing 2017 via online searches. We could cease operations very soon.

What was truly amazing is that we were not the only ones feeling the pain due to the lack of sales. Bobby Dazzler used to be a special place to come to. A place where the owner wanted to eat and sleep in. It gave so much joy and pleasure to be a part of this retail business. It was the first love of my life. It came before the hubby and kids. It give so much pleasure and fun in life that it became a part of the personality. It was a way of making a living without even caring if it made money or not, never wanting to go home because it never felt like work. However, it eventually started to matter when things shifted. How could that same place that had been so special, be loathed now? It was due to the unusual events, shifts in buyer behavior, circumstances and issues. How is it possible that the very place that gives you wealth, money, a livelihood and passion would eventually make you feel so tired, beat and absolutely done!? It was time to go. Going crazy to figure out what could be done to improve sales was not an option, as we were, personally, done! It cannot be positive to work in a place where there is constant bullying around the corner daily to make life miserable. The lease ceasing came at the perfect time for Bobby Dazzler. Not only was the retail apocalypse well underway but the problems and issues of feeling stuck in the "retail jail" just wouldn't let up. Doing something for that long takes focus, resilience and determination. Knowing when to let it go means that Bobby Dazzler had outgrown being a retailer. It was time for change. That change was a major shift in thinking. It was a shift from being a materialistic retailer who conquered all the financial goals towards a path of a spiritual healer. Something that aligned with the soul that would be much more fitting. However, before going into that story which would have to be another book, general challenges that retailers faced are discussed ahead.

GENERAL RETAIL CHALLENGES

HABIT

So, what caused the retail world to go through this massive shift? Many, many different factors came into play that changed consumer habits for good. These habits were compounded with the external forces that could not be controlled by any retailer. Society had completely changed in the way people spend money, spend their time and the way they sees malls, stores and the shopping experience. The apocalypse was going to be inevitable. Some of the different changes in consumer habits and the external forces that shaped the retail world will be examined in the following chapters. Retail as it was known in the past was not just being re-shaped by changing consumer tastes but also by changing attitudes towards the store experience.

BASIC

As we rummage through glossy magazines, newspapers, books, and online pictures of homes or real estate for sale, we are able to see homes that are clean, basic and are based on the principles of minimalism. Billboards and other forms of advertising all clearly point to homes that are picture-perfect with very little stuff inside them. Getting organized, closets that are very easy to access and in order means that we have less in the homes than what used to be. Could it be all those cable or Netflix shows that provide us with images of living with less? Or it might be that homes are getting smaller. Apartment/condo living is quite condensed in big cities like New York, Toronto, Los Angeles or London. People are just living more and acquiring less.

What does this all mean for retail? Well, if homes are being shown with very little clutter in them, then the clutter and stuff that was normally purchased at retail stores and brought into our homes is no longer the "in" thing to do. The trend is toward clean lines, basic living and de-cluttering the homes. It is not just a trend either but stylish to live with little rather than buying more and more "stuff" to make our homes look too busy. So when we are continually being shown pictures of clean homes with little in them then we as the general population pay attention to this and just buy less; we collectively think before buying and go to the malls less. Basic living also means that customers who once used to focus on making purchases are now focused on aspects of life that society has placed importance on.

BRAND

At the retail level, it was hard to believe that the bare basics started to have a brand all of a sudden. Underwear, socks and water all had a brand name. However, as consumers started to shift their habits, the desire for the brand was sought after by the rich and not the lower classes. The middle class was being eroded slowly and that was most evident with the demise of the department stores which actually catered to the middle class. Retail was either brand name, house brand named or no-named.

So, many brands were affected by the retail apocalypse which started to gain momentum. Major brands started to see an impending retail ice age coming upon the world. Michael Kors was one major brand in the United States that announced in 2017 that they would be closing down 125 locations in the next two years. They are a major brand that operates 827 stores. Coach saw a downturn in the handbag industry also, and started to close stores down three years ago. These closures are a major hit as many brand-named retailers try to innovate their retail experience and to bring a re-birth to their products. Without going into each and every single retailer that is downsizing, closing or declaring bankruptcy, the brand names clearly took a hit. Demand for the brand just declined. Many stores saw foot traffic decline, mall traffic slow down and consumers choosing alternatives to past obsessions with brand-name items. Sure, the rich, wealthy and ultra-rich still could afford to purchase brand-named items but generally retail presence in every mall was not as necessary as it was once was. It didn't matter which brand it was, major brands saw a shift in buyer behavior towards their wares.

Clearly, all brands were being affected by the sudden retail downturn. Iconic stores like JC Penny, Sears and well established Macy's which carried an assortment of brands were finding it difficult to survive and were distressed. Brand-named retailers simply opened their own stand-alone stores that carried a much larger selection of the brand's full lineups. Department stores seemed to only carry a limited selection which thereby caused clients to purchase from the brand retailers that were operated by the companies on their own. Hence, a doubling up of retailing took place. Michael Kors brand handbags may be purchased at a department store or at the actual

Michael Kors stores. Most consumers chose the Michael Kors stores due to a better selection, variety and clout. Department stores faced sales declines in each and every single brand that they carried. Brands like Nike, Adidas, Browns and so many others all opened up retail stores and outlet stores of their own so that the consumer had more choice, variety and sometimes lower prices. It became a no-win situation for the department stores. Retail was sinking so fast in 2017 that over 300 US retailers had already filed for bankruptcy at the time of writing in 2017 and that is a staggering 9,000 stores which would be closing by the end of 2017. It was predicted that up to 25% of the shopping malls in the US would close due to the retail apocalypse by 2022. It didn't matter what brand it was. The retail bubble was bursting right before our eyes. The retail fail included all brands and all sizes of retail, big or small. No retail brand was infallible. Even the very biggest were affected.

HOARD

There was a time when it was cool to collect them all, add to our collection or the customer was told not to miss any of them but that all changed when it became uncool to hoard. Hoarding is good for the retailer and de-cluttering is not. After all, if the customer doesn't want the latest, newest and the best right away then retailers and retailing starts to fail. By 2018, the desire to hoard more "stuff" by making more and more purchases for stuff seemed to have declined significantly. It could be that we had collectively stuffed our closets silly, packed our homes up to the hilt, then crammed our garages as much as we could and then even found some self-storage units to put some more of our stuff into. G-d knows what is hiding in all those self-storage units all around town. It was insanity in humanity. Society that was trained to believe that you "never know when you will need it" - even if the stuff is 30, 40 or 50 years old. Yet we all know you never need any of the stuff that has accumulated in the closet, the house, the garage and the self-storage lockers/unit if we haven't used in the last 2 or 3 years. It is all about the "just in case" that the conditioning in our mind keeps replaying. This is clutter; it is not cool and de-cluttering is in so that means hoarding is not. This nonsense was getting out of hand for all people. Why were we keeping things that no longer serve us? Because we were told to, old thought patterns, conditioning and the inability to let go.

Bobby Dazzler started to pay attention to some businesses that were doing exceptionally well. Junk removal companies like 1-800-got-junk were making inroads in the business world, in a very, very big way. Bobby Dazzler also saw that once the junk was gone, clients were NOT replacing it anymore with more stuff from retail stores. This meant that de-cluttering was in and retailing was out. Customers were learning to let go of stuff and even starting to share their stuff. Sharing stuff is discussed separately below.

Hoarding was just not as stylish as it used to be. The words "let go", "let it go" and just "donate it" was the new cool. This was not good news for the retailer. Once people called the junk removal companies, it wasn't like society was running back to retailers to fill their closets, homes, garages or storage units up again. Humanity was seeing it as clutter and that junk was expensive to remove out of the house in the first place or costly monthly to keep in storage units. Why not let others use it before it gets obsolete? It made more sense that people use that stuff NOW or at least while others could.

Using the example of buddy Dave whose parents kept each of their seven childrens' room in the exact same way after each child moved out. The beds, mattresses, dressers, nightstands and all the other stuff in the room are never touched or used again. That was 40+ years ago. When Dave's parents passed, nobody wanted the beds, the mattresses or any of the furniture. Not even for donation since it was outdated, obsolete and were not even usable for charity anymore. They had simply kept the clutter way too long for it to have been useful. Dave said that he called ten different charities and attempted to donate all of it as goodwill. Nobody picked it up, claiming that it was junk! Meanwhile, Dave's parents who were 88 and 89 felt there was value in them keeping all the stuff in each of the bedrooms, "just in case." Or if someone wanted to use the beds or furniture. At the end of the day, Dave said that it cost him more $10,000 to get rid of stuff that should have been given away years ago when someone could have actually been able to use it. This applied to all the stuff in the house that Dave's parents lived in. Stuff that was purchased in retail stores. Nothing was of any use, even as a donation. Dave paid the mega bucks to get rid of the "junk" so that he could put the house on the market as nobody made any offers with the outdated "clutter" in it.

Bobby Dazzler even saw many book store retailers started to carry books that helped people to live better lives by de-cluttering and that means buying less. Some notable reads were:

The Year of Less How I Stopped shopping, gave away my belongings, and discover life is worth more than anything you can buy in a store

The Joy of Less: A minimalist guide to declutter, organize and simplify

Living with Less: An Unexpected Key to Happiness

Living with Less: The Upside of Downsizing your life

What's Mine is Yours: The Rise of Collaborative Consumption

Essentially, hoarding was frowned upon so much that cable television and Netflix came up with shows that viewed hoarding in a negative manner. Some of those shows are:

Hoarders

World of Compulsive Hoarders

Hoarding: Buried Alive

Clean House

A & E's: Hoarders

When shows such as these take off, the likelihood of collecting more stuff over at the retail stores goes down. People just started to live in a more basic way, as described in the earlier chapter, *Basic*.

Additionally, it was no surprise to see that the share economy had taken off. Retailers were also seeing new economies emerging and gaining traction, such as the gig economy, the gift economy, the barter economy along with the largest growing share economy. This could have been due to the next generation of thinking which was making the share economy grow at an ever-faster pace. Retailing was getting harder and harder not just because many clients were waking up to the fact that thrift-store shopping was becoming "in style" but also due to the fact that to become more green meant buying less. New retailers were emerging such as ThredUP, Gwynnie Bee, Rent the Runway, Vinted, Snob Swap, Poshmark, Material World, Swap, Grailed, Refashioner, Ebay, Tadey, Vestiarire Collective, just to name a few online ones, but there are actual bricks and mortar stores also. People are into sharing what they already own. This extended into our areas of life such the sharing of cars, bikes and homes with the rapid development of :

Airbnb

Evo Car Share

Modo

Car2Go

ZipCar

Mobi Bike Share

The above just a few examples from Vancouver, BC. Retailers of bikes and cars are sure to take it if this share economy continues to thrive. There are many, many more examples of share business that are flourishing and are causing the retail world to take a hit. This was also elevated with online website such as:

Craigslist (an online flat form where people can buy or sell)

Close5 (eBay)

Oodle

Facebook Marketplace

Geebo

Sell.com

The above websites and networking sites are just an example of where individuals could buy and sell used or new items that people no longer needed. Clearly, hoarding is connected to the retail sales plunge around the globe. Thus, by 2018 the retail fail can be attributed to some extent to the desire not to hoard which really translated into not going shopping at retail stores as much.

HOURS

Everybody knows that in order to make sales, we need to open for business. But that makes retails hours long and really horrible. Retail is open every day with the exception of Christmas Day in Canada in most locations. This may be similar to the United States. This is one of the hardest parts of the business. Yes, we are open on New Year's Day in some malls in Canada. Who knows why? The first client doesn't even stroll into the store till 2-3pm in the afternoon. Usually, that client is hungover from the previous night of partying and looks like they have not even gone home yet. At least that is what they smelled like. Yuk! Time to get out the air freshener! Retailers keep ample supply of this stuff for those kinds of days or for those stinky customers who forget to take a shower before coming to the mall. New Year's Day was an utter waste of staffing, energy and time. Sales were pathetic on this day plus it was hard to convince staff to work that day since they were out partying the day before. New Year's Day became a draw out of the hat as to who was going to take the shift. Yet major malls wanted the retailer to be open for more sales.

Owning a retail business means that you are in a retail jail when it comes to the number of hours the stores are open. Retail opens up typically at 9:30 am and goes till 6 pm or 7 pm on Monday or Tuesday. Wednesday through Friday, the mall hours are normally till 9 pm. Saturday hours are shorter, being 9:30 am-6 pm or 7 pm. While Sunday used to be closed in the past, but now is open from 11 am-6 pm or 11 am-7 pm. Retail hours have slowly been extended over the years. Stores are starting to stay open till 9 pm even on Mondays and Tuesdays in major malls. This doesn't necessarily mean that shoppers wanted the extra hours. It just meant that landlords did see sales slipping away so the only way to hopefully counter this problem was to extend the hours to make sure the customers have enough time or more time to shop. These extensions have made it grueling for retailers. Finding staff to fill in these extra hours or having to pay overtime just made it that much more difficult for the retailer to make a living from the retail business. That is why retail is nicknamed retail jail. There are so many hours that one has to be available to the business that when a retailer is on their feet 10-14 hours per day, it feels like jail not work. Retailers definitely have it tough when it comes to super-long hours.

Those hours get extended when Christmas comes so that more people come in later. The mall stays open till 10 pm, 11 pm and sometimes till midnight. Larger retailers have even further extended their hours by staying open 24 hours day like 7/11. Some Shoppers Drug Marts and some Walmarts go all night long selling. It should also be pointed out that even when a manager or owner goes home, the retail business is still on their mind after hours. So yes, the retail business is a really time-consuming business in terms of the number of hours that are spent. Hours outside of the store include time spent researching new products, looking for ideas to improve sales, planning monthly goals and quotas, buying, accounting, and just worrying about the store without even knowing about the hours that are spent in thought. Wow! Sometimes it felt like there was NO time to sleep, just retail 24 hours, 7 days a week. These hours were only extended with the advent of online sales through cyberspace, which is discussed elsewhere in the book.

Cards

There are many different forms of payment for retail goods and services. Some of those forms of payment were discussed in scams. However, cards, specifically gift cards, were seen by the retailer as the perfect gift. They were meant to be a no-hassle way to gift so that it was easy to wrap and ship. They eliminated the whole decision-making process, which thereby also eliminated the whole retail shopping experience as well. Bobby Dazzler accepted mall gift cards and credit card company-issued gift cards but only issued gift certificates at the store level. Our store did not have a Bobby Dazzler gift card program.

Gift cards were interesting in that many who purchased these used them for services like restaurants, grocery stores, coffee shops, electronics and other activities. However, gift cards didn't increase traffic in the malls due to many people purchasing gift cards for more practical daily things that people needed or enjoyed. Retailers like Bobby Dazzler did not really benefit as much from the introduction of gift cards. Gift cards made it possible to give a family a grocery gift card rather than an item or product from our store. Gift cards changed the way people shopped. Prior to 2009/2010 gift cards had an expiry date so if the gift cards went unused then the gift card was void. However, after bringing in new regulations for their use in Canada, fees were attached to them to extend the time limits to use them.

But this still didn't eliminate the possibility of the gift cards never being used. Many clients simply forgot about them and never bothered to pay the fees associated with reactivation of the gift cards. This forgetting about the gift cards did impact the retailer in a great way. If the clients weren't coming the malls to use the gift cards, the traffic wasn't declined. In addition, when gift cards are actually used by the consumer, they generally spent more than the value of the gift cards. However, that would not happen if they forgot about them all together. This forgetting about the gift in the wallet attributed to about one third of all gifts cards purchased going unused; a very significant amount. Consumers spent $130 billion US in 2015 on gift cards according to CEB, a professional services firm, that was noted in an online article about unused gift cards that are lost but not forgotten.

It should also be noted that the $130 billion of gift cards are not necessarily purchased in retail stores. Gift cards are sold in gas stations, grocery stores and drug stores which are actually all places of convenience. Retailers do not get that traffic, convenience stores or grocery stores do. Retailers rely on the browse around, look around and social crowd that helps to push sales when clients used to come to the retail store to purchase the gift cards. Having them available everywhere doesn't help add-on sales, sales in general or foot traffic. Sure, the retailer collects the money and considers it pure profit but there are consequences in the future for the retailer due to the clients not returning to use the gift cards. Consumers normally spend more than the gift value and if there is a small balance left on gift cards the consumer does end up spending a lot more than the small dollars left on the gift cards with balances on them.

Forgetting prevents traffic, fewer up sales, fewer profits and adds to the demise of the retail world, especially for goods that are novel such as those that Bobby Dazzler sold or for the department store sales. In other instances, retailers love gift cards that go unused due to the fact that the money is in their bank and if a client doesn't ever use the gift card then retailer is in a win, win situation. They have the money and no goods or services have left their business.

GREEN

The green movement has gained traction due to the awareness of global warming and desire to preserve Mother Earth. Humanity in general is starting to pay attention to the excess plastics being thrown into our oceans, garments being disposed of in our landfills, and the extra stuff bought at retail stores that is disposed of after just one use. Retailers are, in fact, one of the biggest culprits and contributors to the destruction of Earth. The fashion industry happens to be one of the most environmentally onerous industries on the planet due to the novel nature of fashion. We choose to wear something for a little while when it is in style and then dispose of it. After going on the H&M website, the company even admits that the fashion industry which they are a part of is using more resources than the planet allows. This can be found easily with a quick Goggle search.

But, H & M is making strides by choosing to become leaders in the industry by introducing textile innovation using a minimum of 50% 'conscious' materials.

At the retail level, consumers purchasing aimlessly just to have the latest and newest is an unrealistic approach to being green. Thus, the going green movement definitely had negative side effects when it came to the retail world. Clients started to buy less due to their desire to pay attention to Mother Earth and be mindful in the manner they shop. Clients second-guess purchases now more than ever. The green movement undeniably hurt the retail sector without a doubt in a very significant manner but in a positive way coming from an ex-retailer. People actually started to think before making a purchase. This was not so much the case in the early 1990's. The green movement took a bite out of retail sales from a different angle. The client started to come in by 2017 saying that if it "ain't broken then there's no need to replace it" or "let's see if we could get on Craigslist" or "let's check out the thrift store like Value Village." Natually, this green-movement traction put a downward spiral into retail sales. Retailers couldn't just get away with whatever they wanted to, like in the old days. Taking an initiative was now a part of retailing. Even governmental regulations got tighter. The malls all had recycling areas for all waste that the entire mall created that needed to be separated properly. The "C" Center had three recycling areas where store waste was separated further into bins that include plastic, cardboard, batteries, e-waste, electrical, bulbs, packaging, glass, food recycling and much more. Recycling was the new way.

Since Bobby Dazzler was a retailer of novelties, it appeared that the novelty of an item wore out quickly so it could easily be disposed of. Sometimes our items were only good for one party or one time use since they were party favors. From a personal perspective, the desire to sell more "useless" stuff was no longer aligning with the personal choices and the choices of society. This was definitely not a sustainable business anymore. Clients were becoming very cautious and very aware of each purchase. More and more of them were becoming involved in the green movement themselves at home, in their business and in life. Clients were becoming mindful and conscious of their decisions. It was almost futile to push a sale when the feeling was the same from a personal perspective. It was becoming clear as day as time went on for Bobby Dazzler and for many other retailers that we were selling "landfill waste" that caused harm to Mother Earth. This made the sale even harder to make when a personal shift in attitude came about. Becoming more conscious, aware, awake and alert to the needs of Mother Earth doesn't help a retailer to continue in the same manner as they once did. Clearly, the green movement started to resonate with the owner of the business who just couldn't do that anymore to our precious Mother Earth. It became a personal shift in thinking.

Vices

As the years went on, Bobby Dazzler noticed that the clients were paying premium prices for items that were related their vices. Vices are habits such as smoking, drinking, partying, drugs, food and sex. We simply found that the motto of the store "unique and innovative" no longer served us, so by the year 2002, we re-branded the Bobby Dazzler stores to be "got what's hot!" That was exactly what we sold by the time late 2002 hit. We moved away from expensive gadgets and moved into the $25 and under range of novelty along with party stuff that included smoking, drugs (ganja), drinking and sex. Our focus changed with the changing needs of our clients. This was a major shift for the store but a very, very positive one as the store became the mall's go-to place for party stuff. It was nicknamed the sex, drugs, and rock-and-roll store. Items such as wine glasses, barware, smoking accessories, bongs, pipes and bachelorette party favors made over 65% of all sales. The last 35% was novelty, seasonal and trend items. The majority of the sales from 2002 to 2017 centered on the categories that we referred to as vices. However, by 2017, ganja products sales accounted for 60-70% of all sales from January to September. This category of sales was growing far past all the other items in the store. This growth mirrored what was happening in society. Sales in ganja-related accessories, paraphernalia and the actual "ganja" itself were growing but other product sales were declining. The sales of these items also explains the explosion was of sales that was going on in the world of the medicinal marijuana business. It was affecting retail sales without a doubt.

GANJA

Ganja is another word for marijuana, pot, mary jane, weed and medical marijuana. It is smoked medicinally by many but some use it recreationally as one of the vices to relax with. According to a quick Google search, Forbes magazine puts the sales of marijuana in North America to grow from $5.4-billion business in the U.S. in 2015 to $16 billion by 2020. Meanwhile, illegal marijuana sales are estimated at $40 billion according to a Vancouver Sun article on May 9th, 2018. Cannabis tax could reap $112 million annually for British Columbia, Canada, so it is a very lucrative market consultants predict. These figures could be higher, of course. And those figures are increasing at unprecedented rates of 30+% per year. It should be kept in mind that the figure is for the legal market not the illegal markets which would be billions more. Black-market marijuana sales made up 87% of all pot sales across North America in 2016. The black market captured $46.4 billion dollars. That is a huge amount. And not all illegal pot will eventually be legal.

The growth of online sales has not been nearly as "high" as the anticipated growth of ganga for the years to come. Online retail sales have gone from 1% in the year 2000 to 8.3% in 2016 according to online articles published by Zero Hedge in 2017. This is definitely an increase but the numbers are much higher for growth for medicinal marijuana. The numbers don't add up. Pot, weed, grass, ganja, medicinal marijuana is inevitably taking a very high percentage of sales that is not being accounted for as it is gobbling up retail sales. Getting high is an experience. With the advent of medicinal marijuana, more people are thinking it is normal and mainstream, just like drinking booze or wine. These are things that are shaking up the retail world that have not been taken into account previously.

The large gaps of missing percentages and dollars are all money that might have been spent in the malls at retail stores. Those are consumer dollars that might have gone into the purchase of items or products that Bobby Dazzler and many other retailers sold. Medicinal marijuana is one of the biggest oversights that retailers missed when wondering what was causing the massive retail apocalypse. It is impossible not to explore the possibility of marijuana being a consumer product that well customers are going to buy to get high off to feel good instead of buying more tangible goods. Marijuana is part of the experiences that people enjoy. It is a feeling experience! And it appears that these experiences are being enjoyed a whole lot more if the industry is hovering around the $6.7 billion mark or more.

Making ganja legal makes the whole notion of using it normal. Shoppers Drug Mart in Canada has applied to sell marijuana right beside all of the other normal, everyday items that people buy like milk, eggs, butter and toilet paper. People will be able to throw some pot into that basket too now. Wow! It creates a domino effect that happens when a hot item hits the market. Using the most recent 2017 retail craze, the fidget spinner, as an example, one is able to see just how wild the craze was. Before we all knew it, every Joe Blow had one and was looking for one. Once one person had it then the whole world wanted it. Ganja is not different from any other commodity. Consumers use it and may sometimes abuse it by using it recreationally. However, the dollars that might have been spent at retail stores are now being shared with the legal and the illegal marijuana markets in North America. The more it is available, the more it is going to be smoked plus the more it will be considered normal. The more normal it gets, the less people will frequent the malls and retail stores, spending their money instead on the getting high on ganja experience while at home on their sofa instead of being at the malls or in stores.

The exception for Bobby Dazzler was the smoking accessories/ products associated with marijuana. Those sales sky-rocketed after a trial run in 1997. It was 1997/1998 when Bobby Dazzler experimented with one of the locked showcases to retail smoking accessories. Smoking accessories include products like lighters, pipes, cigar pipes, cigarette cases, bongs, rolling papers, grinders, rolling machines and all the other paraphernalia associated with smoking everything. It was cutting edge for the time. Everybody who came in asked, "Are you able to sell this stuff?" Well, yes, they are all just smoking accessories. There is nothing illegal about it. We sold so much from this one showcase that we expanded it to two cases within a year. Actually, if we could have changed the entire store to smoking then we would have made a mint. However, all leases have clauses and we signed up to be a novelty retailer of gifts, gadgets and gizmos. So, changing the entire store to smoking accessories only would be a whole new retail concept. Items related to smoking ganja did phenomenally in sales. Mark-up was great and profits were huge. A glass-pipe purchased wholesale for $1.50 could fetch $12 to $15 easily. That is easily a thousand percent. The smoking section was added to the selection of Bobby Dazzler items that we would carry permanently, right until 2017.

Sales in this category started to take off so fast that during the months of January to September, we had found a category that did so well that the two showcases paid the rent easily. Smoking stuff carried the store and during the seasonal months of October, November and December the focus shifted back to gifts, gadgets and novelties along with the sale of smoking accessories. However, as some more years lapsed, a shift in buyer behavior occurred whereby customers focused on all their vices and less on the "stuff" that they brought home. The vices again related to the experiences that consumer was into. Marijuana was part of the high. Clients would simply bee line to the back showcase to pick up their smoke paraphernalia and leave. It was popular for ages 19-70+. All age groups loved to smoke pot. Smoking and drinking were part of relaxing and get a little or a lot more buzzed in the evening after work. People loved to relax!

A final note on ganja was the immense amount of money that many companies who had successfully obtained the medical marijuana license were able to obtain from investors who believed that ganja was the next great thing. Marijuana was supposed to become legal by October 2018 in places like Canada. Many companies were raking in dough from investors in the millions who felt that the stock in these companies was only going to go up and up. Companies who held medical marijuana licenses also benefited with the immense amount of capital that they were able to round up to grow and then sell to countries around the world such as the EU. This, again, impacts retail sales. If investors are investing in pot stocks then there is less money to put into the purchase of goods at the retail level. Funds are diverted to stocks of ganja companies instead of into the inventory of Bobby Dazzler stock.

DEBTS

Did anybody really have money? The United States never quite got over the great bailout of the banks from 2007-2008 and the sub-prime mortgage failures of 2007-2009. Americans buckled down tight and changed the way they spent their hard-earned cash, and attempted to keep the debts at bay. Those tightened budgets and the managing of debts meant that habits of restraint when it came to money would continue. Americans were not going to lose their shirt again and go through another crisis. Canadians were carrying record levels of consumer debt too. The same can be said of the dangerous household debt that the Americans are currently carrying. According to CNN *Money*, consumer debts levels are flirting with levels that were similar to those in 2008, $12.68 trillion by the end of 2016. This is incredible!

People are bombarded with sky-high mortgage loans, car loans, credit card loans and even tuition loans for school. People just don't have money to throw around on "stuff" that Bobby Dazzler or other retailers were trying to sell. Things were getting tight by mid-2017 and everybody was looking at their household budget despite the economy being in an "upward" swing according to politicians. The actual day-to-day playout of the economy did not appear to be on any upswing nor was the mood of the average client who complained about debts. Debts and debt prevent people from spending more money on extra "stuff": extra stuff like novelties that nobody needs but everybody wants. It was a hard place to be in for retailers in 2017 with all the consumer debt. Some days it just felt like retailers had to pull teeth to get money out of their clients. This was felt across the board.

Trump

Retailers have always wondered why elections are held just before the largest selling season of Christmas. In 2016, a major political upset in the United States of America not only caused uncertainty there but also all around the world. In Canada, our clients were so shocked that it became impossible for them to focus on spending any money at Bobby Dazzler. In fact, clients would simply come in and complain about Trump being the new President of the United States during the busy 2016 November and Christmas selling seasons. His name was on everybody's lips and the focus became Trump not Christmas shopping. There was truly a level of political uncertainty that created a non-confidence in the consumer, so much so that it felt like we needed to pull teeth even harder to get our clients to spend money.

Retailers did suffer from the new political landscape that had emerged in the United States. This uncertainty caused the US dollar exchange rates to plunge near the end of 2016 and right into early 2017, a situation that was obviously not good for retailers like Bobby Dazzler who made all their inventory purchases from the United States. The possibility of NAFTA (North American Free Trade Agreement) being cancelled only worsened the woes of Canadian retailers since that meant inventories/goods coming from the United States could cost even higher on top of the ridiculous US exchange rates that we faced. The political upheaval only added to the problems of the rates. By mid-2018, not much had been achieved in terms of the retail sector, as a result of Trump being the President of the United States. Bobby Dazzler felt confident that the correct decision has been made in exiting the retail world. Many of the items that our retail store sold were subject to higher tariffs and duties which meant that the retail prices of these items would be higher.

Costs

The general costs of operating a retail store were soaring by 2017. The costs to renovate or build out a new store due to construction costs were sky high. Everything was costing so much more than it did in 1990. Costs like:

Legal Costs

Accounting

Payroll

Insurance

Business Licenses/Permits

Group Employee Benefits

Advertising

Rents

Credit/Debit Card Fees

Banking Fees

Inventory - 90% of the Bobby Dazzler store was being purchased from the United States by 2017. The US exchange rate was 1.304 in January 2017. The exchange rate does not include shipping to a customs broker, brokerage fees, duty and taxes which all need to be added to the costs to arrive at the actual cost for items from the United States. This renders it almost impossible to order and actually be able to sell products at a reasonable price in Canadian dollars. This was a huge problem for the Bobby Dazzler retail business on top of all the other expenses and issues of running a profitable retail business.

It should also be pointed out that as costs for the retailer increased so did the costs of living for the average consumer. The middle class were experiencing higher costs for shelter, foods, transportation and living expenses which thereby meant less money to spend at retail stores. The costs of living do impact the consumer level to such a degree that the retail level feels an immediate impact.

TECHS

As time went on, tech, which is short for technology, became the evil villain of retailers who were trying to work with a bricks and mortar store concept. Techs allowed the client to access cyberspace while they shopped in bricks and mortar stores looking to make a purchase. Sure, there were benefits to having a phone, tablets and a computer for the retailer but old-school retailing had changed forever with the advancement of the phone for checking prices, sizes, styles and online shopping. This was just the tip of the iceberg.

Retailers had to deal with clients who would talk on the phone while talking to the clerk at the same time. How rude! Do people actually think that it is okay to just pick up the phone while the sales clerk was in middle of a sales pitch for the hot, new item that was being so energetically shown to the prospective buyer. Clients would text and call while the clerk was trying to speak to them on a face-to-face basis. Clients would simply cut the clerk off on ALL OCCASIONS because ALL calls were important no matter what. Even those that started off, "hey what's up?" There was no discretion left nor were there any manners left. People just thought that it was okay to rudely answer the phone while this clerk was making their sales pitch.

It got worse after that. If a sales clerk actually got past the sales pitch, the client would actually call up a dozen or so friends to see if would be a good idea to even make the purchase for the product or not. If nobody answered, the client would Facebook, Twitter or Instagram all their friends to see if the item would be suitable to purchase for themselves or as a gift. The client could not make up their mind by themselves, they needed the advice of their friends or family. The client would no longer be able to just "buy it". This was definitely a growing concern for a small novelty business that relied on impulse sales. Techs ruined the sales of Bobby Dazzler by making people ask their friends, family and even acquaintances if they should make the purchase or not. Indecisiveness increased ten-fold. The sale was lost once the input of another person was thrown into the sales pitch. Hence, techs made all clients indecisive and unable to make a decision on their own. There was no more self-reliance left. All purchases needed to have some sort of consultation through the handy techs that were in their pockets all the time, namely the cellular phone. And, if nobody answered their messages on the phone or through other means of social media, the client would state that "they need to come back" after they consulted with the rest of the world if it was okay to make the this $20 purchase. Really?! Frustrating for sure!

If a client did come back, which they did sometimes, they showed some class by letting the sales clerk know that they would not be making the purchase due to the item being found online for a cheaper price. So the techs made the retail bricks and mortar store a showroom store for all the online retailers. There is something wrong with retail if the small business is paying the rent, carrying the inventory and yet not making the sale because the item can be found online cheaper than the retail price at the bricks and mortar store. Why are we even bothering with retail? There will always be cheaper prices online no matter what. The way humanity is conditioned is that we should always look for the cheapest price and not care about our loyalty to a retailer. All that matters is price. Well, online retailers in most cases will be cheaper because often they are not paying the sky high rents of $12,000 per month like we were. Online retailing is much cheaper to run on a monthly basis due to hosting and other fees that never equate to operating an in-line store with rents, staff, inventory, utilities and all other expenses that come with keeping an in-line store in the malls. There will never be a way to compete effectively with the online retailer who is going to undercut the brick and mortar store with no problem. Look to Amazon and Ebay as examples of this scenario. They have collectively taken major bites out of the retail world. Department stores find it extremely difficult to compete with the likes of Amazon who are able to offer delivery fast and prices that so difficult to compete with.

So it became clear that bricks and mortar stores were slowly becoming showroom stores for ALL online retailers, only there was no financial benefit forthcoming by continuing to do this. Bobby Dazzler got tired of being the model/showcase store for those selling the same item online for a cheaper price. The problem with being a model store for online retailers is that Bobby Dazzler is NOT making the sale. The sale is being made by the online store by using Bobby Dazzler as a showcase store that is paying rent, paying staff and stocking the item for nothing. The products in our store were just a model for the online items. This is not a business model that works for a retailer for very long. It can never work because there is no loyalty left for the retailer, only cheap prices matter.

People would damage a product by touching it, feeling it, using it and trying it. Worn products don't get the same money as new products do. Using the example for costumes, customers would try on Halloween costumes, check the sizes, the fit, the price and then simply order online as it was much cheaper. Meanwhile, the retailer just allowed the costume to be tried on, manhandled, possibly even be stretched, subjected it to some wear and tear, the possibility of damaging or ripping it with it having a worn/used look to it without it even being sold. Price match would have an option but some of the retailers were actually selling the same costume for $2-5 cheaper or higher than wholesale, making the whole notion of operating for a profit a circus.

The next problem that technology brought to the retailer was that staff would constantly be using their techs while at work. This caused staff to be less efficient in sales and in undertaking their duties of running a retail store. Staff simply spent time on Facebook, Twitter, Instagram or Google rather than selling in the retail store while being on their phones. It was impossible to watch for this or keep track of as staff who were left to take care of the store once the Store Manager or Owner went home. Sure, rules were put into place that the phone must be in the back while they working their shift but this was very difficult to monitor. The temptation to abuse this rule was always at play. Thus, techs took the efficiency of staff away. Techs were hard to control as virtually all staff had phones. One could not simply tell their own staff not to bring their phone to work. The use and abuse of it for personal reasons was out of control in the retail world.

DIETS

Having a discussion on retail without talking about food is like having a mall without the food court. The food court for a mall was the busiest place in the mall. After all, everybody has to eat! Right! Yet, something was definitely shifting when it came to humanity's desire for food from the food court and their diets! Not only did traffic taper off, due to the numerous other reasons that are discussed, but the food court was no longer the hangout spot that it used to be. The food court is still the busiest part of the mall but people were becoming more health conscious so that means the fast foods like burgers, hot dogs and fries that once attracted the customers are no longer as tasty an attraction as they used to be.

Client tastes had evolved to healthy foods that take into consideration calories. In Canada, restaurants were required to post exactly how many calories their items had right beside the advertised items on their menus and food boards. This naturally caused many people to take a look at what they put into their bodies. Most food court vendors in the past had been the typical deep-fried foods that were not viewed as healthy by Health Canada, nutritionists and dietitians all over the world. Naturally, as leases lapsed in the food court for those who carried fried foods, healthier choices were brought by the landlords into the food court. This improved foot traffic somewhat but fresh, healthy and nutritious options were more expensive than fast, and still not as good as home-prepared meals. It should also be pointed out that the rising costs of meals also made it cheaper to bring meals from home. It was actually starting to become stylish to brown-bag a lunch daily not to mention a whole lot cheaper. When this started to take place, the "C" Center took the communal microwave away from the center of the food court in order to discourage retail employees from warming up their own food. This was most likely in the hopes of having staff in the malls purchase food from the food court rather than bring it from home. Bobby Dazzler simply purchased their own in-house microwave and didn't leave the store anymore after this took place. This is when we all knew even the food courts in the malls are hurting not just the retailers. If the food court starts to hurt then there are some real problems brewing in the retail world. Food courts are a draw, as everyone needs to eat. Right?!?

However, there were some ways the food court could drive traffic to their centers. Food courts could adopt the whole "appy hour" promo from 2 pm-5 pm. Many full-service restaurants have appy hour every single day in order to drive traffic to their establishments during the non-peak times between lunch and dinner. This has worked wonders for a variety of restaurants. It's not surprising that the food courts in all the malls have picked up on this. It would certainly bring some much needed foot traffic in, plus it might even draw some of the usual clients that visit full-service restaurants inside of the malls to eat at the food courts or any other restaurants that operate in the mall. The food court could also offer delivery to the stores around the malls. This was something that was never implemented but as retailer that often did shifts on my own, it would have been really handy to have the food court offer a delivery service to the stores that order via an app or by phoning. Many of the food court workers were quite quiet during the non-peak hours of 2 pm-5 pm and those would be great times to offer delivery service when one of their staff is just standing around. It would have been a win-win situation for the food court retailer that just increased their daily sales and for the retailer that could not close down the store just to make a food run that might take up to 15-20 minutes. Stores really weren't allowed to close down unless it was a washroom break. Some retailers such as ours did not have a small bathroom in the stockroom, so we had no choice but to take bathroom breaks. But taking a bathroom break along with a food break could take up to 30+ minutes of a store being closed which was not acceptable. That food coming to the store would have really been a nice service. Perhaps these types of ideas can be implemented now in order to draw more traffic and sales for the food court clients who are having to deal with clients that are watching their diets. Everybody has skips or cheat days and so the food court could offer appy hour deals to help sales.

The next issue which is related to diets is sport. Not only were clients watching their diets but customers were now working out, doing a sport or two, starting to take care of themselves better, watching their health, taking measures to prevent disease and actually becoming mindful of what they were eating. *Diets* was also related to the topic of *Sport* which is discussed next.

SPORT

People were just not going to the mall as often as they did in the past due to clients deciding to focus on their health by doing a sport instead. Personal fitness, health and taking care of the self were becoming more important than buying the next new handbag. That is why Michael Kors and Coach were both downsizing. As a retailer who sold so many novelty water bottles in the last five years, it would be an understatement not to mention all the clients who came into the store with active-wear. There was obviously another social change that was taking the sale away from the retailer. The rising number of Yoga studios, the number of fitness centers, the number of people using personal trainers, the popularity of dance classes like Zumba, the 24/7 gyms that opened up all around town, the number of people cycling and basically the rising number of people who were working out was noticed. This impacts retail sales. The sales of not just water bottles but also t-shirts, hats, shorts, workout pants and the many other items/products that clients take with them to the gym all seemed to go through the roof in sales.

People were partaking in sports, exercising more, doing more walks, more yoga, more biking and generally spending a lot more time doing sports but not shopping. Sports is broad. It includes many activities like Karate, Jui Jitsu, Taekwondo, Kung Fu, soccer, hockey, jogging, dancing and all outdoor sports. Society was changing its whole attitude towards shopping. Instead of spending time walking aimlessly, wandering the mall with the sole purpose of either wasting time or making unnecessary purchases, there was an alternative. The choice to work out and take care of themselves was obviously taking precedence over shopping or "pigging out" in the mall food court. Doing sports relates to health. Since many diseases like stroke, heart attacks, diabetes, high blood pressure and cancers were rapidly increasing in numbers, consumers felt the need to take better care of themselves. Humanity was raising its consciousness. The consumer was simply paying more attention to their health rather than wasting their wealth on acquiring more useless "stuff". The momentum to do more sports and take care ourselves is only going to increase not decrease. This shift in buying behavior obviously had a detrimental effect on the retail world, so much so that the dismal retail sales resulted in a prediction that 25% of the malls in the United States would most likely close by 2022.

Malls took notice of these lifestyle changes that society was implementing. Malls were even bringing gyms and fitness centers in to spaces that were vacated by retailers that sold wares. Malls found a new way to bring tenants into their malls. They lured the consumers who now focused on their health and well being by installing state of the art fitness centers in malls. It was a great way to repurpose the space for use in a functional and profitable manner. So, the large landlords were fully aware of the changing habits of humanity.

LARGE

Bobby Dazzler had to deal with large business on many levels. There were large governmental organizations for the collection of taxes, landlords who leased the spaces to Bobby Dazzler, large suppliers who sold products to the store, large financial institutions who took care of the finances for Bobby Dazzler, large competitors, and large credit/debit card processor companies just to name a few. By 2018, some large show business names like Bill Cosby, Harvey Weinstein and Kevin Spacey had already been exposed with their dirty secrets that related to abuse and sexual harassment of women. It was time to expose the large business corruption that Bobby Dazzler experienced.

Bobby Dazzler being a small retailer needed to expose the abusive nature of large businesses that it dealt with over the years. Whistle-blowing is always difficult because the large always do business with the large. It became apparent in the business world of the small retailer that the large would often bully the small. Some of the problems and sufferings that we experienced were discussed earlier in the section on personal challenges. However, the large businesses were definitely not playing by the rules all the time, which always makes it harder for a small retailer to stay in business.

The downturn of the retail apocalypse was not just affecting a small retailer like Bobby Dazzler. The large were also suffering and this included department stores, landlords owing malls, brand names with a large number of stores and even some large big box stores. Now the downturn in the economy resulted in large swathes of retail spaces becoming vacant at the expense of the large landlords who acted in a heavy-handed manner towards the small.

Without going into every single retailer and outlining what each one was losing, some examples will be looked at for clarification. The large, major retailers suffered as well such as J.C. Penney, RadioShack and Sears who all went bankrupt in 2017. Canadian retailers like Sobey's which runs the Safeway chain were feeling the pinch. They sell food. That can make one worry for sure. A quick Google search reveals just how sales were going for this food retailer. Large retailers like Canada's beloved and long-term retailer (Hudson's Bay Company), also known as HBC, have reported massive losses in the past two years. Those loses include a steep fourth straight quarter loss of $152 million dollars. Those losses are continuing right into 2018. In order to create a much more balanced portfolio, the company has made decisions to sell off some of its hard real estate assets in order make up some of the losses, transform and restructure. These were all reported online and be can found with a simple Google search. And then it was reported that another loss of $221 million came about in the first quarter of 2017. Which happened to be double the size of the loss experienced in 2016 for the same quarter. With losses of this size, it is very difficult to see large retailers that have been so powerful and successful for years continue to eat up such large losses over and over again, quarter after quarter.

Iconic Sears, a large department store that has been around for 65 years shuttered its doors and planned its bankruptcy towards the latter part of 2017. Toys"R"Us filed for bankruptcy protection in September 2017 and then went into full bankruptcy in 2018 due to the enormous amount of debts it was carrying. Who would have ever thought that the largest toy retailer would go out of business? But they did in the United States and in the United Kingdom. Were children no longer playing with toys? That may have been one of the problems with this retailer. However, the woes of Toy"R"Us started due to it having huge overleveraged debts that made it impossible to stay afloat. The interest payments were so high for the debts it was carrying that its operating cash flows were unable to meet the interest payment obligations. Many department stores also started to restructure, downsize and close inefficient stores such as JC Penney, Macy's, and Target, just to name a few of the large ones. Another 3,000 stores were due to shutter in 2018 and the full list for 2018 can be checked out by doing a Google search of your own.

Again, this book is not about printing out graphs and stats, those are available online and viewed with simple Google searches. It is only a matter of time before even the most successful and large-sized retailer realized that retail may be not just be going through a major transformation but an actual apocalypse. Bobby Dazzler may have been just a small retailer but we paid attention, careful attention, to what was going on around us as the retail apocalypse started to unfold. Many retailers were told that this too shall pass, but it really didn't, it just kept on going. Business leaders and malls were coming to their wits' end trying to figure out what was actually going on here. Where had all the sales gone?

On the plus side, Bobby Dazzler had been bullied by the large landlords for some time. The rise of the empty shops did provide Bobby Dazzler a sense of feeling good due to the negative karma that the large malls had sowed by throwing the small independents out. The large do suffer, too.

In 2016, the landlord who just couldn't find a space for Bobby Dazzler in a mall amongst 550 units at "M" Mall and was part of the lawsuit almost 10 years earlier even attempted to lure us back to another property they owned in a new mall that was opened up close to United States border. Some great perks were offered to induce us to come back; however, once the large mistreated us in the manner that they had in 2007, we would NOT want to do business with them again nor take a chance at being treated like their doormats again. We knew who were dealing with. It is not a joke as the email is being provided below with the names removed to protect privacy and to keep the mall anonymous.

In 2018, Canada's own Tim Horton's was going through a significant amount of "business suicide" by treating their franchisees in an unfair manner. These disputes are obviously causing damage to the reputation to the very large, proud Tim Horton's. Meanwhile, Starbucks was also in some hot water by calling the police on two black men who were just sitting in one of their stores in Philadelphia without ordering anything while waiting for another business partner. Loblaws along with some other large grocery stores were engaged in bread price fixing by as much as $1.50 per loaf for the past decade in Canada and this was uncovered late in 2017. In order to make this up, the company was offering $25 store credit but the catch was the consumer had to hand over some private details plus agree to their Terms and Conditions along with the beloved Privacy Policy. Alas, nothing is for free, there is always a catch, right! Large corporations making decisions of the type described above cannot possibly continue with the same upward momentum.

Some ways the small could avoid all the chaos was to avoid doing business with the large. The small could return to the small mom and pop coffee shops to purchase their morning coffee. This would support the small businesses and the small people. Bread can be purchased at the small, family bakers who don't overcharge for their bread nor care to engage in any pricing fixing of the most basic of commodities, breads. The small can simply pay attention to other small businesses to change their buyer behavior to support businesses that care and those that are fair. The small will start to pay attention and actually start to disconnect from the large. The small must keep their self-respect in order to carry on.

STATS

S tats is short for statistics. Retail stats are available online but this book is not focused on the number-crunching aspects of retail. There are plenty of stats available online for this. To realize that a retail apocalypse is going on, one only needs to visually see all the empty storefronts, vacant malls and the vacancy signs all around in so many cities in the United States and Canada. If a detail of graphs, charts or other data is required, that is readily available via a quick online search. This book will not be engaging in any actual number crunching. The reader is able to access those themselves. This "reveal all" is meant to provide the reader with an experience from a small, independent retailer's point of view with general information. This provides an overview of challenges that retailers face on a personal, small level and on the general level from the perspective of a small retailer in the world who competes and operates alongside the large retailers and national companies. Stats are also available in other books that discuss how to survive and thrive in retail. Some of these books are based on studies and based on research rather than on a personal perspective of one retailer. Some great reads on that subject are:

Delivery Happiness: A Path to Profits, Passion, and Purpose by Hesish

The Design of Everyday Things by Don Norman

The New Rules of Retail: Competing in the World's Toughest Marketplace, by Robin Lewis and Michael Dart

The Reality Check: The Irreverent Guide to Outsmarting, Outmanaging, and Outmarketing Your Competition by Guy Kawasaki

Buyology: Truth and Lies about Why We Buy by Martin Lindstrom

The Paradox of Choice: Why More is Less by Barry Schwartz

The Retail Revival: Reimagining Business in the New Age of Consumerism by Doug Stephans

Retail Business Kit for Dummies by Rick Segal

Loyal

Large retailers offer loyalty points when consumers shop in their stores such as Airmiles, Aeroplan, gifts, free merchandise, notice of sales first to preferred clients, preferred client discounts and many more ways to develop loyalty with the consumers. Bobby Dazzler was a small retailer. We just knew each of our customers and could give a discount when a regular came into our store to shop. We kept a call list of great clients who would be called when new gadgets would come in. We knew our clients by first name and even knew what they had bought last. Bobby Dazzler gave "free" gifts with large purchases and was generous with making a promotion for a client who dropped "big" money. Being an independent retailer meant that we had leverage and the ability to change prices for anybody. They just needed as ask and then it was given. It was that simple; we wanted to sell.

Having this social interaction and human experience is what retail used to be like. It is the way that mom-and-pop stores like ours grew. It was because Bobby Dazzler was able to offer a personal experience. This meant that our customers in 1990 were loyal. Once they shopped in Bobby Dazzler, then they always shopped at our store. Clients were happy to find additional locations later, as well. By 2017, nobody was loyal any longer since clients become more fickle and became very price sensitive. Any brand-named item such a Guess handbag could now be purchased in many places, not just at the Guess store or the department store. Anybody could become a retailer. There were so many more retail stores and malls that over-retailing was actually killing brand loyalty. Clients could go to a department store, an outlet store, online line and the actual store that sells just that brand. Clients were given so many choices that there was no need to be loyal anymore. Malls lacking in diversity also make clients less loyal to the retail stores.

Suppliers were no longer loyal to retailers. In the early 1990's, suppliers were loyal to one retailer in one mall to carry the items that they sold. By 2017, due to so many more retailers being around, suppliers started to sell to so many other retailers that it become cut-throat. Products one store had could be at the competitor's store, in a kiosk, online or at the department stores, who bought directly from the supplier without the middle distributors or the sales representatives that took a cut from the wholesale that they sold. Suppliers even started up their own websites so that they sold their wares along with the retailers they sold to. There was no loyalty to the retailer. Using the example of colored contact lenses that Bobby Dazzler sold, our supplier sold the contacts at retail prices that were $5 cheaper than our retail price and provided free delivery from Montreal. Bobby used to sell 500 colored contacts in the three weeks leading up to Halloween. But now that type of commitment seemed exaggerated given that we had to put our order in for the quantity we desired by May. Why would Bobby Dazzler bother ordering 500 colored contacts as we normally did for Halloween if our own supplier had them online for $5 cheaper. This is not being loyal anymore! This is nonsense retailing.

The owner (landlord) was not loyal to the retailer anymore, as put forth with numerous issues of having many retailers in the mall carrying the same wares. With greed comes money and the desire to have more retailers to make money off of. Bobby Dazzler had a 10 year lease with the last landlord. However, this did not stop the owner from bringing in the main competitor of Bobby Dazzler. It also didn't stop the landlord from bringing in a cart/kiosk that carried colored contact lenses for the Halloween season. Nor did the owner think twice when they signed up a pop-up/temp store to sell costumes alongside a long-term tenant who has made financial and inventory commitments to the center to the tune of $1.6 million dollars. Frustrated, unfair and lack of loyalty are the kindest words that Bobby Dazzler could come up. The same scenario occurred again when the landlord decided to bring in temps during Christmas to carry some novelty items that would bring further sales declines to Bobby Dazzler. The loyal landlord was long gone. It was all about need for greed.

Loony

People had gone loony over the loonie stores. In Canada, the loonie is the name for the one dollar coin that we use as legal tender. It is referred to as the loonie while the two dollar coin is referred to as the toonie (or twoonie). The one dollar stores in Canada are thereby referred to as the loonie stores. Bobby Dazzler felt the impact of loonie stores right away. In the US, these stores are called Dollar stores. Loonie stores carried party items, novelties and seasonal product for just $1 or a little over that. These retail prices were lower than our cost prices due to the very low volume that we purchased at compared to the very large dollar stores. They had multiple locations, large warehouses and import contacts from overseas (China) that Bobby Dazzler could never compete with. Loonie stores even took sales away from general stores, drugstores and grocery stores. Their products were really inexpensive plus they were very busy so turn-over of product was high. Oven mitts were just $1.00. A black toque that did not have a brand name on it was just $1.00. The comparison at the department with a brand name on it was $29.95. Wow! This is not a small difference if the consumer doesn't care about the brand as discussed previously. People just wanted cheap stuff and the quality was half-decent too.

Who would have thought that creative retail like Bobby Dazzler would be replaced by stores carrying items for just $1? Nobody would have thought that these retailers would become department stores' competitors either. These stores were cheap stores carrying made in China junk yet were growing like wildfire. Despite having a hard winter during the 2016 Christmas season, stores such as Dollarama were growing and gaining strength in the market at unprecedented rates.

While the dollar store sales rose, the middle department stores plummeted. This was largely impacting department store sales which saw the decline of the middle class.

They were not only fuelling an economy with inexpensive items but were servicing the lower class with their wares along with hiring staff that were paid low wages or minimum wages. Thus, the lower socio-economic class of the Loonie Store was a growing segment at the expense of the middle class which was shrinking along with the middle class retailer like Bobby Dazzler or department stores.

Dollar or Loonie stores appealed to everyone since they carried stuff that everybody could afford. But generally, they appealed to the lower socio-economic classes that still thought that shopping was cool and acquiring more stuff was life. The death of the middle-class buyer meant that a large portion of shoppers who frequented middle- class stores like Sears, Macy's, JC Penney and other brick and mortar stores simply vanished. The retail pendulum had swung up towards the upper class that didn't care to go loony at the loonie stores but would rather make a quality purchase than multiple purchases that are $1.00. High-end retail was actually taking off. These types of retail stores were usually in downtown areas or in higher end malls in urban centers. Many malls catered to the middle class which meant that suburban malls were the ones that would be hurt the most. These loonie stores were not only making the mall seem cheap but essentially devalued the shopping experience. These stores impacted Bobby Dazzler in a very significant way as they carried many seasonal items that retailed for a much higher price at our store. The dollar stores were able to carry party and seasonal items for so much cheaper. They were definitely giving us a hit during Halloween and Christmas. Little items that we used sell in mass were no longer popular since they were sold for so much cheaper in the dollar store. Most malls already had price-competitive retailers like Wal-Mart to give Bobby Dazzler competition but the dollar stores were coming in droves. Some even arrived from Japan and China into the Vancouver markets that had large Asian populations.

The "C" Center already two dollar stores in it by 2017 and one very large one across the street from the mall. The Bobby Dazzler store was slated to be replaced by yet another dollar store that was considered higher-end dollar store concept from Asia. This meant that items could be higher priced than $1.00.

The loony behavior only continued with loony business decisions being made by large corporations. The greatest business blunder made by a business had to be the decision to take Target into Canada. Target came into "C" Center by taking the formal Zellers store there. After almost a year of renovations, taking up crucial parking spots during the Christmas season and causing so much noise, construction, and disruption to all the retailers in the complex, these guys pulled out of the mall less than two years into it. Why would anybody think that Canada with a population of some 35 million plus or minus in 2013 could ever support a middle-class retailer like Target which opened up 133 outlets all at once in an aggressive manner when retailing was already having issues in Canada and the United States. This was a clear lack of planning. Did anybody do the numbers? Sears, which was also in many malls and also in "C" Center was having many struggles in sales. Adding another player into that retail segment seemed to be a no-win, no-brain situation. Having so much retail that competed with each other didn't make sense and retail that was more expensive than the already established Shoppers and Wal-Marts in Canada had to have had a loony leader to decide to move forward with this.

WAGES

After rents, wages are the second biggest expense for the retailer. Wages pay for staff, group benefits, bonuses and any other benefits employees receive as compensation for work performed. Bobby Dazzler experienced wages climbing from 1990 to 2017 but retail sales did not increase in the same manner, according to the Government of Canada's website.

Minimum wages in British Columbia in 1990 when Bobby Dazzler first opened were $5.00 per hour. Minimum wages in British Columbia for 2017 were $11.35. This means that wages more than doubled in those 27 years. The United States experienced a similar trend.

Wages in 1990 were approximately $3.80 per hour and in 2017, the wages were $7.25. This is not quite double. However, retail sales did not double nor had productivity of the staff. In fact, retail sales have been steadily falling since the meltdown of 2008. It has been very, very challenging to see payroll expenses rising at a rate that has an inverse relationship to sales in many retail stores. From an independent retailer's point of view, the only way to deal with this was to keep payroll low by having only one trusted staff member working during non-peak periods of January to September. This not only saved on payroll but actually made the staff more efficient in running the retail store profitably. The staff member was expected to shoulder the daily quota, complete the list of tasks and run the business with no other person to fall back on. It was found that having two people on during non-busy times not only decreased efficiency due to the unnecessary gossip, jibber jabber and chats that took place among the staff members while clients were actually neglected when the conversing with each other took precedence over sales, approaching clients, and carrying out the general daily retail duties. It was determined that once a quota was left for a staff member who was working alone, the quota was actually met. The staff member reserved chats and conversations to the customers rather than with each other. That was their only outlet to chatting so they actually approached clients. Staff felt the need to impress and meet goals when they were given shifts by themselves, plus a level of trust that was placed in them gave them confidence. It should be pointed out that our business was only 1200 square ft., so this may only work with smaller retailers. But not necessarily with larger retailers. Staff also could not blame poor sales on the other staff member since all sales were in the hands of the one staff member. This method of scheduling kept payroll down and helped to make sales quotas.

Bobby Dazzler had additional expenses to the payroll such as the employer's portion of the EI (Employment Insurance) and CPP (Canada Pension Plan) that is a mandatory expense. In order retain our employees, Bobby Dazzler also paid into a group plan so that full-time and some part-time staff were able to receive medical and dental benefits. Yes, the group plan was very expensive but it encouraged staff retention and allowed our staff turn-over rate to be low.

TEMPS

Temps is short for temporary stores. Temps are retail stores that set up shop on a month-to-month basis for short-term leases. They are temporary retailers that don't have long-term commitments with the malls. They are short-term rentals that come in to retail during the peak seasonal periods or other times of the year. They are also referred to as kiosks, or pop-up retailers today. They pop up and then go away. Pop-up retailing seemed to be really taking off in the 1970's when the first kiosks came to be. There are many benefits to operating kiosk such as lower overhead, small inventories, low or non-existent CAM (Common Area Maintenance), tax, utility expenses, and marketing fees compared to the in-line stores Bobby Dazzler had to deal with.

Other temps and pop up retailers come to be as a result of empty retail stores being utilized by the landlords. Landlords who were unable to fill spaces up with long-term tenants simply leased space on a short-term basis to retailers that came for peak periods or those who wanted to try out new products before taking the plunge to sign a long-term lease. Bricks and mortar retailers view the temps as a major rival. However, these rivals are brought in by the landlord who usually took the cream and the extra profits that could have been the long-term tenants'. The main problem with temps from a retail perspective is that there is no point to committing to a mall. Landlords will simply bring in as many temps as possible to take the razor-thin profits that are already being split with the actual competitors in the mall.

Temps were simply a pain for a novelty retailer such as Bobby Dazzler. Novelty retail is such that it relies on peak selling seasons like Halloween or Christmas so that it makes it almost impossible to project what the retailer should order. Typically, a retailer like Bobby Dazzler must place their order by the end of February for a Halloween order that arrives in August-October. However, landlords do not advise the retailer if there is going to be a pop-up store that will be competing with the exact same products an inline retailer will be carrying. Thus, the chance of over-ordering and underselling becomes really high due to the pop-up stores coming along in October-December to cash out in high season sales by taking the cream off the seasonal sales that the inline retailer would have anticipated being their own. The temps or pop-ups were definitely making life impossible for the regular bricks and mortar retailer.

The loyalty the landlord had to the long-term tenant was definitely gone with the introduction of so many temps and "pop-up" stores. However, this competitor was one that the landlord would knowingly bring in just to earn extra rent at the expense of one of their own inline retailers. This particular situation made it a NO-win situation for the long-term, committed retailer, who would not get the same commitment from the landlords. The landlord was not able to understand that there was room for only one or two carrying Halloween costumes or accessories in a suburban mall. In 2016, Bobby Dazzler ended up selling all the costumes at 50% off with three weeks left till Halloween in order to remain competitive with the "pop-up" stores and the online retailers. This resulted in dismal profits for 2016. A total sabotage of seasonal sales hampered the desire to carry on with retail as it once was amplified by these temps.

TAXES

The bricks and mortar stores were also challenged with the fact that internet sales were not on an even playing field when coming to taxes. According to a 1992 ruling from Quill v.North Dakota, focused on mail order and catalog purchases, requiring that a business must have a physical presence within a state in order for the state to collect sales tax. This made internet sales non-taxable in many cases since many businesses had an online presence only. The 1992 decision was obviously obsolete for the e-commerce era. This decision was only overturned on June 21, 2018 by the US Supreme Court. The new ruling, maintains that internet retailers can be required to collect sales tax in states where they have no physical presence. This new broader law on taxing will enable government tax authorities to reap from $8 to $23 billion a year in tax revenue. The ability to collect these amounts in taxes shows the type of edge over the bricks and mortar stores that the internet businesses had all this time. Sure, the playing field is leveled out a bit but the clients still have gotten used to the idea of shopping online instead of going into stores. This tax correct does come but it may already be a little late for retailers who have already closed.

RENTS

For a retailer, the largest expense when running a business or store was definitely the rent. Rents in 1990 were manageable. Bobby Dazzler started at rates of $15 to $20 per square foot in high traffic malls. Even those rates were lowered when we moved to a new undeveloped location in 1995 due to our not requiring as large a space. However, just as real estate prices and inflation shot up in Canada so did the rents. This same could be said for the United States and many other countries. Rents became sky high, especially in high traffic locations like Robson Street which is considered the Rodeo Drive of Vancouver. A 600-square foot store could cost as much as $8,000 or more per month to rent on this street and about half that amount in a number two mall. That rental amount did not even take into consideration payroll for staff, utilities, and other expenses associated with running a store. This seems really cheap when compared to the astronomical rates that some location in United States stores paid. A Google search (on Wolf Street) shows that commercial property has been affected by the exit of some many retailers. In some cases, retail store rents are plunging.

However, rates on Fifth Avenue between 49th and 60th street in New York which are considered prime areas are $3,116 per square foot which is a whopping US$3.1million per month for a 1,000-square-foot store. And Bobby Dazzler was complaining about CND$12,000 per month for the same square-footage in a suburban mall in British Columbia, Canada. The sales have to be amazing to get these rents and other expenses paid. It may be an extreme example but the point is rents were really, really ridiculous. The commercial market is definitely hyper-inflated. Some landlords are waking up to this reality that units may sit empty for years if their pockets are deep. But an astute landlord would be able to see the trends and make adjustments in order to have a retail space leased rather than it being vacant. Sure, a landlord is able to wait for the right tenant but with so many spots becoming available, that wait can take a long, long time.

At one point, Bobby Dazzler did get up to five locations in four malls along with running a kiosk at the YVR (Vancouver International Airport). Rents for all locations soared past $65,000 per month. Wow! Sometimes it was hard to believe that there were good days when retail made so many sales to sustain itself and support a staff of 20 people. It was a family business (mom and pop) that actually got to a multi-store level.

Unfortunately, as time went on it was impossible to carry on with multiple stores and make a profit. That was due to the changing scene of retail and the transformation that started to take place with the introduction of big-box Costco, expansion of Wal-Mart, and other larger stores that carried everything. The two profitable stores seemed to carry the two money-losing stores. So, as the leases lapsed and rents never went down, the money-losing stores were closed down. It appeared that the sky-high rents did not take into consideration the growing a number of retailers doing the same thing, the advent of online sales and number of other social and economic factors that are discussed in this book that made rents crushing for a small retailer. Rates on Robson Street soared past $130-$175 per square foot by the 2000's. Who in the world can afford these rates and actually do business with a profit? Well, the large businesses such as Nike and UGG could afford to keep these stores as their showcase stores. But small retailers simply could not afford the pricey rents and were basically driven off of Robson to side streets that were cheaper. But, that only lasted so long until real estate prices got crazy everywhere. This meant that rents on side streets were also crazy for small square-footages.

By 2017, Bobby Dazzler was paying a monthly rate of $11,000 for a 1,000 square-foot store in the slower part of a suburban mall which was located 30 minutes outside of Vancouver. This is the equivalent of paying $132,000 per year just in rental remittances plus % rent. It must be kept in mind that the rental remittances do NOT include payroll, utilities, licenses, insurance and the many other expenses that go along with running a small business. Plus, an inverse relationship started to exist with retail sales to rents. Sales were going down and rents were going up due to many issues, as has been discussed.

CYBER

B obby Dazzler jumped into the online business while having the bricks and mortar store in 2007. Costs for setting up an e-commerce website are astronomical for a small retailer. Some webmasters/designers provided estimates as low as $1,500 to a high of $25,000 to set up. We were just a small retailer and wanted to have an online presence as soon as possible since this was just the trend for a part of the evolving and successful retail business according to all "industry experts." Luckily, in 2007, Rob, a friend came back from Norway and was trying to make a name for himself in the web design business. On a simple handshake, he agreed to set up the e-commerce site as his first project with no upfront costs to Bobby Dazzler other than hosting, having a merchant account and/or PayPal account for business transactions. He was provided with free artistic expression for the online part of the Bobby Dazzler business. The site was nice and fully functioning by late 2007. Online sales did take place and were usually 2-3.5% of in-store sales. These percentages only fluctuated between 2 to 3.5% from 2007 to 2011. Updates were made to the products that we had in-store to our website by Rob during that time period since he also benefited from the sales due our agreement to provide him 10% of all net sales. The nicer the website and the updates, the more sales which would thereby lead to more commission. It was supposed to be a win-win business agreement.

By late 2011, Rob started to refuse to update the website under the oral/verbal agreement that we had. He indicated that he wanted $75.00 per hour for updates since it took all of his time. By now he was working on many other sites that paid much more, namely porn sites and sites that had no content, whatever that was supposed to mean. He indicated that the Bobby Dazzler site was just peanuts compared to porn and that is where the money is. He even boasted that some of the sites that he ran/operated just took a client's credit-card number and didn't even have content or products that were being shipped out. This is when Bobby Dazzler realized this guy was just trying to squeeze more money from us for updates when online sales were so weak. The biggest year we had in sales was $8,500 and that included taxes. Giving consideration to the cost of goods and taxes, the profit was $3,795.65 and of that we needed to give Rob 10%

which was approximately $758.92, leaving us a profit of $3,036.73. And Rob wanted $75.00 per hour on top of the 10%. Doing the math and time spent in the line-ups at the post office mailing these packages out was really NOT worth it for our business. After not agreeing to give him $75.00 per hour for updates, Rob took the site down without our knowledge as he felt that he should be getting paid for the updates. Not only did our website go down but our friendship was over at that point. There was no point to work with this guy if he could take the drastic measure of taking down our site. He also claimed that if I accepted his offers for dates with him that he might have been able to work things out. Um, no thanks! He was trying to screw us like all other people on his porn sites. No pun intended! Like many in the past have said, it is never a good idea to go into business with friends. Well, lesson learned again.

There were other serious issues with the online business that many don't realize until a fully operational e-commerce site is running. Sometimes, when a client placed an order for an item or multiple items on our site, they would suddenly put a dispute in with PayPal within one minute of placing the order. PayPal would then freeze those funds until Bobby Dazzler responded to the dispute via PayPal and provided the required documents to PayPal that the items were shipped out. Not only did this cause extra time, energy and chaos to the day, the client also called up asking for the tracking number within minutes. There was no patience in any of the clients. They would email, then would call, and we would be dealing with a $20 sale, which was just a pain. This might have been due to many clients getting burned with online purchases in the early days whereby an item is paid for and never arrives. However, during late 2007-2011, the time spent engaging with clients who demanded to know the tracking # for the shipment was a daily nuisance. Clients wanted the information immediately. It was not what Bobby Dazzler anticipated with respect to sales in cyberspace.

Clients assumed that Bobby Dazzler operated in the same manner that Ebay and Amazon operated and expected the same level of service in relation to speed and response. Bobby Dazzler does sleep and we don't service clients 24/7. Clients also threatened to put negative reviews of our business on their Facebook, Twitter and Instagram accounts. But we didn't have any of these cyberspace social media accounts and saved ourselves from all this chaos. There came a point that we actually questioned if online sales were worth all the hassle. This was ridiculous! Bobby Dazzler felt that in order to be an efficient site and online presence, there needed to be an IT guy/gal hired. However, sales were not high enough to warrant this expense so we just sucked it up till our relationship with Rob fell through. We even thought that it was a blessing in disguise. There were issues with the web-designer and clients when looking back to online sales. After the e-commerce went down, we simply replaced the site in 2011 with an information-only website and focused on the sales at the store level.

Cyberspace retail proved to be a little challenging for the small, independent retailer. By 2017, the online hype encouraged retailers to be competitive with pricing. Well, that sounds all good but in reality how could a small business sell items that their own supplier sells online? Hence, suppliers were competing with the retailers. They already have a shipping department so why not just use them to have a website and sell one or two pieces at a time. Using the example of the Minecraft t-shirt that our business got for US$10.00 wholesale and retailed for C$25, the actual supplier would sell the t-shirt for US$20.00 on their own website. If one purchased two, the second was half the price.

Next, competitive pricing does NOT make any sense to the small retailer and would not get the same price as, say, Wal-Mart or Amazon. A small retailer only purchases 12 pieces or 24 pieces at the time. The wholesale prices are never going to be the same for a large retailer that buys 100 or 1000 at a time. Using the disco light as an example, Bobby Dazzler paid US$15.00 for this item plus shipping, handling, customs fees, brokerage fees and taxes. By the time this item landed with all expenses taken into consideration, the item would retail for C$39.00 in store. If we had a online store that is the price that we would need to sell it for. That price does include the price of packaging to ship the item in. That would be an extra cost borne by Bobby Dazzler. Nor does it take into consideration the time and energy to go to the post office or have a courier come to pick up and deliver the parcel to a client. A quick Google search reveals that this item from the same supplier retails for US$14.98 in Wal-Mart USA with two day shipping. The iconic Lava lamp was carried by Bobby Dazzler from

1990 to 2017. Our cost for the 14.5" lava lamp which we sold at 150-250 pieces during every single Christmas season was US$15.00. Our Canadian retail price was $39-$45. However, a quick Google search in 2017 shows this identical item being $19.98 Canadian at Wal-Mart and costing only $5.98 to ship. Shipping for Bobby Dazzler is much more than that since we don't have an account that ships out as much as Wal-Mart does. Wal-Mart is able to ship this item out cheaper and sell cheaper than Bobby Dazzler by a long shot. There would be no way we can compete with this at the store level or online. Cyberspace was ruining profits for the small retailer. This is what makes the argument for being competitive with pricing and being online a no-win situation for a small retailer like Bobby Dazzler. Our buying power was just not strong enough.

Being online also takes the whole notion of personal customer interactions out of the picture. Online sales have no personal interactions with clients that are face to face. Clients simply click, pay and wait for their purchase. Online was seen as being convenient plus was easy to use in lieu of personal service. Sales are done from computer to computer. This also means that clients save time by not driving down to the store to go find a parking spot, having to walk into a store and get the item so that they drive back. Cyberspace or online retailing is way too convenient, so much so that a bricks and mortar store can't ever compete with that much convenience.

It should also be pointed out that returns are a major issue for stores like Bobby Dazzler. Being a small retailer of novelty merchandise means that we are unable to take returns, yet some major online retailers take returns back leniently. This is a huge problem. Using the example of Halloween costumes, not only were margins razor thin but the whole notion of the costume being returnable was preposterous. Clients could simply order the costume, use it and return it to us after Halloween. Not only would we be stuck with the costume but there is NO way of knowing if it was worn or not. Many large retailers allowed returns of costumes on top of free shipping. Our wholesale on a typical costume was $39.95 or $41.95 for a great-quality costume. The same costumes could be found online in 2017 for $49.95 with free shipping. How could anybody possibly make any profit from doing business like this? Quick Google searches ruined in-store sales when the client pulled out their phone to check to see what the price was online. So were back to the problem of clients trying the costume on in our store and purchasing it online for cheaper. This was more than frustrating. It was no longer business as usual. Bobby Dazzler was being used as a showroom for online retailers for free.

By going online, it became apparent that the retailer needed to have a product that was unique for that store to be successful. Competing with the world in cyberspace selling items or products that other retailers were picking up, made it virtually impossible to compete with stores all over the world. Retailers were no longer just competing with the rival in their own mall. Cyberspace changed the game in a big way so that a retailer was now competing with the whole world for price, product, customer service and delivery of the item right to their door. Using one of the most popular recent fad items, the fidget spinner as an example, the problem can be exhibited. The fidget spinner came out late December in the United States. It become hot in Canada around late February or March. Our local wholesaler Jimmy, called us up and asked if we wanted some at $8.00 a pop. Meanwhile, eight other emails in May arrived from various other suppliers we do business with each offering the fidget spinner for $4.75 to $5.00 wholesale each. This is a significant price difference from what Jimmy was offering them at. By June, the retail prices of the fidget spinner had tanked to $5.00 on Amazon and Ebay. Not only was the item available in every single dollar or loony store for $2-$3, it was online for even cheaper. By July and August, some suppliers were actually oversupplied with fidget spinners and getting rid of them for $.49 to $.75 each. This is really crazy pricing for any retailer to compete with and still worry about rent, staff and overstocking of an item that almost every retailer in the mall carries including Wal-Mart. The possibility of getting stuck with high-priced fidget spinners would have been very high as we would had to buy 48-72 pieces at time. Retail prices would continue to fall around us but we would be stuck with some inventory that was purchased when the prices were high. There might even be a chance that we would lose money if retail prices fell low enough. Is this what retailing had come to? It was time consuming and energy sucking by 2017, so no wonder it was leading to an apocalypse.

Cyberspace was providing convenience without having to leave our homes. Bricks-and-mortars stores like Bobby Dazzler could not compete with this type of convenience. This was so easy. You order, pay and wait a few days till the door bell rings from the courier or postal worker who would bring your items to your door. This is crazy easy. Large online also provided more than just commodities by going beyond the call of the sale. They could give speed with the number of warehouses that they held. The best example is Amazon, which is so big that a small retailer could not possibly compete with the turn-around time of a monster like this company. Amazon had even gotten into groceries by 2017.

Continuing on with cyberspace also requires a closer examination of just how much time is being spent on the internet at the various sites. Studies done indicate that the US resident spends 32 hours per month of which 22% of the time is spent on social networking sites. This figure is from 2012 so it would be even higher in 2018 at the time of writing. This figure can be found on a Google search by going to "Mind Jumper" and looking at time spent on social media.

Once again, the stats show that people enjoy looking at the screen and aren't bothering to come to the malls or retail stores to have fun, engage, or even shop. They are quite literally using cyberspace as a means of entertainment instead of shopping. It is all being done through cyberspace and accelerating at an alarming rate. This is more than a mere shift or transformation in the way we do shopping. It is a retail apocalypse.

MEDIA

Retailers may have underestimated the impact that media has had on the retailing world. Shopping is considered a pastime. Social media and digital media are both two forms of media that have been growing phenomenal rates as pastimes. Social media sites such as Facebook, Instagram, Snapchat, Twitter and even networking sites like LinkedIn are all seeing their numbers grow at astronomical rates. This growth is fueled by the desire to connect with other people online as a pastime. People are on social media at home, at work, at the coffee shop and while on the go. Their eyes are fixated on the screen, not the stuff that is on display at stores. Consumers who once were fixated on the wonderful displays of the store are now screen-fixated. This fixation is taking a toll on retailers across the board.

Where once shopping used to be an "in" thing to do with friends or family as a pastime, now the "in" thing to do is connect with people, check out people and see what everybody else is up to on social media. This all requires time, and that time is now spent on social media sites that are worth millions and billions of dollars. Their worth is getting stronger since more and more of the consumers that would have been in the malls at retail stores choose to spend time socializing via social media rather than physically going to the mall or retail stores to hang out, walk around or make a purchase. It should also be noted that it is easier to stay home and connect with friends than to get off the sofa or comfy bed, get dressed and go to the malls or a store. Studies don't even take shopping into consideration when looking at how much time people are spending on social media versus the alternatives. This is something that should be examined or at taken a look at by Google: just how much time is spent on social media by Americans and by their Canadian counterparts.

In one study, social media is behind watching television but it is behind eating, drinking, grooming, socializing and doing laundry. Shopping is not even a choice in this particular study. While socially connecting with others, consumers have found that cyberspace allows them do almost everything right from their homes. Consumers can easily hop over to a site to do some shopping or browsing without ever having to leave their homes. It is all convenient, easy and what all people are sometimes even "addicted" to. Still many others are now switching to working from home, not only finding it easier to work from home but also to connect to their friends from home and again at the same time do all their shopping from home. The advent of cyberspace and social media is a two-way street that is causing the prospects of getting more traffic into the malls and stores to look dismal. It is difficult to convince consumers to change their habits when the new way of doing things is through media. Social media is not going away.

So the best way to use social media is for advertising purposes. Ads can be purchased on social media sites that enable retailers to promote their business or their products. This is one of the best ways to use social media in an advantageous manner.

Digital media sites such as Netflix, Showme, Hulu and Movies123 are also gaining traction at very significant rates that obviously affect retail traffic and sales. Consumers who would normally come to the malls are enjoying their programming on demand and being able to binge on their favorite shows without excessive advertisements. This makes more people want to stay home and enjoy digital programming that is exciting, easy and comfortable rather than walking around retail stores. Passing time engaged in digital media has also taken a considerable number of people out of the malls.

It is safe to surmise that the impact of both forms of media have been grossly underestimated by the retail world. Facebook is worth over billions for a reason. People are on it and using it rather than hanging out in the malls as they used to in the good old days. People are choosing to do things differently when it comes to time management. Habits that are currently forming are not those can be easily reversed. The slide in retail sales has to take many factors into consideration. It would be futile not to examine the very large impact that social media and digital media has had on retail sales.

Blasé

" In order to be irreplaceable, one must always be different."
- Coco Chanel, fashion designer

This is an ironic quote from a fashion designer, considering fashion is one of the predominant retailers in the malls. Malls had become blasé for the consumers. The malls became a beacon of boredom, monuments of mediocrity and havens of ho-hum due to their own doing. The power was always in the hands of the landlord. Ultimately, it was their property and they were to lease it to whomever they wanted. The marketing plan for the owners (landlords) was very to easy to foresee. They wanted to cookie-cut all the malls to replicate each other. If one mall had a popular store, the mall in the next city or suburb wanted it too. It has become boring for the consumer as they anticipated each mall simply being the same as all the other ones. Every malls is just vaguely like the next. The mall diversity and excitement had definitely dwindled. Once a winning concept came out, the malls were all over it and wanted one of them in each of their malls.

Taking the Gap store and seeing how they expanded to so many malls is a great example. The same could be said of any winning new retail store concept that emerges. All large malls have one of each of the popular stores in their malls. The small, independent retailers like Bobby Dazzler were the ones that are actually different, unique and innovative and special compared to the large retailers that were everywhere. However, mall management and landlords were actually taking the small and creative retailers out in lieu of the next Teavana, tAmerican Apparel, Aeropostale, Radio Shack or Payless Shoesource. These examples are being used on purpose as they are large chain stores that are either closing or facing bankruptcy. Today, the bigger the chain, the harder they fell. No retailer was unaffected by the downturn of retail. By 2017, 8,640 stores have closed and more were coming. These figures were taken from quick online searches.

Generally, there have been chain stores who came with a bang and left like a bomb. Teavana was scheduled to close all of its locations, 379 locations. This is a significant number especially if leases are with a single, large landlord who holds many Teavana leases. Naturally, landlords may find themselves having to fight back against such massive closings, which leave huge pockets of empty retail everywhere in all malls. It should be pointed out that over the years many, many small, creative retailers were told to hit the road to pave the way for these exact chain stores who are now crashing. These chains were given a chance to flourish off the backs of the small retailer like Bobby Dazzler. Small retail such as Bobby Dazzler that had previously held so many of the coveted spots had chains take them over in the 80's, 90's and even currently. Small retailers were simply pushed out in favor of large chains who desired the spot held by a small retailer at any cost.

Landlords that own the some 1,200+ enclosed malls helped to cause this blasé movement on their own. They did this in order to secure a new concept which would lure more clients into their complexes. Well, once a small retailer's lease came up for renewal, the landlord did not care if the small retailer had been in the complex for 17, 25, 30+ years, in the same spot and relied on the retail business as a means of livelihood. The small retailer was simply pushed out of the spot so that the larger, upcoming and new retail chain could take that very spot. No matter what! This was particularly the issue when large companies that held multiple locations were looking to expand with a certain square footage in mind and also with the excellent location on top of that. This was experienced first-hand by Bobby Dazzler at "M" in 2007. This was detailed in the sections on *Shawn* and *Sue'em*. The Bobby Dazzler store was replaced by a lingerie chain store despite our being able to pay the same rent or even more just to save the business, the location and our livelihood. This all fell on deaf ears when the General Manager indicated that our complex just doesn't have a spot among 550 stores for your small business or plan. Not only was the landlord acting cocky but added insult to injury by stating, "Is it even worth it for us to consider another spot for you?" Ouch, this not only bites but makes one rethink why anybody would want to go into retail business when dealing with such unfairness and with such unprofessional attitudes. More on that in *Ethics* and ethical business practices.

A part of being blasé for the retailer is being able to find the identical item in multiple retailers around the mall. The nice brand-named handbag could be purchased from the brand-named store but could also be found in the department store in the mall or even at the outlet center across the street for even less. A quick Google search would then provide the consumer with the same handbag online for even cheaper. So, retail was becoming blasé on so many levels since so many other retailers were selling the same item. It was no longer unique to run to the mall and find a unique handbag. It was readily available everywhere, and everyone wanted it online. This thereby made owning it less desirable and so very blasé.

The worst thing that the landlords have not be able to learn from the above is that once the multi-chain store fails, they all fall down at once. At the time of writing, Teavana which is a Starbucks company, would be closing all 300+ stores by Spring 2018 due to low traffic at their locations and in the malls. The nightmare of the bigger they are, the harder they fall, was now transpiring for the blasé malls. Now that is a whole lot of empty spots all at once which is collectively causing havoc in the retail apocalypse. Other problems cited by consumers with respect to the malls was that there were too many teens hanging around the malls, loitering, not buying and too few or hard-to-find restrooms. Malls needed to up their game in a big way in order to get away from the blasé.

Malls have started to become enlightened to the whole concept of malls becoming shopping "experiences". Experiences that cannot be found on their phones, computers, or ipads. Malls are having to change the way they do business. Some malls have put in fitness centers in order to bring those clients who are working out or like to exercise. This is a growing trend. Bringing in more restaurants, movie theatres and other experience based tenants helps to bring a new attraction to their center. Perhaps, it would be good to adopt the idea of a swimming or wave pool like the one found in West Edmonton mall where parents can shop and the kids can enjoy the water, with a lifeguard of course. This is going back to the idea of having amusement parks and arcades in the mall to draw traffic in. However, both of them draw children, tweens and teens to the mall which again defeats the purpose of getting relevant traffic and not loitering traffic into the malls. Other ideas include:

Indoor mini golf center
Hybrid bowling alleys and restaurant area
Dodgem car track
Pool room with tables and bar/grill
Pizza buffets with entertainment

Gyms/fitness centers

Bring back the creative, unique and innovative retailers like Bobby Dazzler who were once "kicked out" for the chain-store expansion (after all, the landlord still has the monthly reports for our stores and knows that rent was paid)

Strictly brand-based stores that are interactive such as the Lego, Barbie or Apple stores

These are just suggestions that landlords can implement in order to make their centers fill up again. Following the social trends of society allows the malls to go from being blasé to fun again. However, big changes are needed to have this happen and that means not adding yet another dollar-store retailer to the mall.

ETHIC

Ethical business practices ensure that the playing field remains fair and equal, with all parties involved following the rules. Ethics are needed in all business but the retail business needs it even more on so many levels. If large business is supposed to set the standards for the small businesses to follow in their footsteps, then they have certainly done a horrible job. A very profitable retailer, Apple, the first example, shows just how unethical large retailers have been. Everybody loves their iphone and buys them, making this company one of the richest in the world. They are slick and beautiful until one examines the production side of the business which is dark, horrific and unethical to say the least. One of Apple's main manufacturers is Foxcann and it is referred to as hell on earth. Conditions in this plant are so miserable that "anti-suicide nets" had to be installed beneath the windows after 17 employees leapt to their deaths in protest of the horrible things they had to do on a daily basis. Tiny child slaves are a norm and are forced to work dangerous conditions with cancer-causing fumes for 10 hours per day, seven days a week. Living quarters are like tiny college dorms in a gigantic beehive-type factory each crammed with crappy bunk beds. Exhausting hours, humiliating discipline, unreasonable workloads and pressure to reduce overtime that results in lower paychecks are just some of the unjust problems. However, this has not stopped Americans and the West from buying the iphones. Beside the Foxconn fiasco, Apple's co-founder, Steve Wozniak claimed Apple was engaging in unethical practices by using an Irish tax loophole to avoid paying billions in taxes on the all their international sales.

Walmart, the world's largest retailer, is vehemently anti-union, in favor of high profits and lower wages. They are a large retailer that is getting larger and larger off the backs of all Americans and others. They are notorious for providing wages so low that full-timers still have to rely on food stamps and welfare to get by. The working conditions also don't fare so well, either. There are issues surrounding non-investigated sexual harassment in the workplace, denied sick leave, reduced working hours and a vehement opposition to those attempting to form unions. Many people dislike Walmart's business practices. Upon entry into a new town, it is almost guarnateed to eradicate all of the small businesses in the area due to predatory pricing that no mom and pop store can survive. It simply destroys business. This was observed when Walmart came to a mall where Bobby Dazzler was retailing. The small independent stores just started to disappear leaving, so many vacant retail spaces behind.

Each of the companies below have been implicated in using sweatshop labor or been involved in other unethical manufacturing processes:

- Forever 21
- Loran Jan
- Quicksilver
- Calvin Klein
- Roxy
- Tommy Hilfiger
- Tree of Life
- Lowes
- Lululemon
- Gap
- Dotti
- Jacquie E
- Just Jeans
- Portmans
- Metalicous
- Billabong
- Victoria's Secret

And so many more that are not even listed above, these are a sample taken from the Sweatshop list on the website: Live Fair Ethical.

Bobby Dazzler as a retailer in British Columbia, Canada, found that here the Commercial Tenancy Act only has 30 Sections which were established (1996) that are heavily favored towards the landlord. The Residential Tenancy Act which was updated in 2002 has 117 Sections. Tenants cannot just be thrown out or evicted just because the landlord feels like a "change". The protections that have been provided to the tenant in the Residential Act are not being extended in the same manner in the Commercial Tenancy Act. The Act is quite frankly flawed and favors large business doing business with large business. Obviously, this is NOT ethical business. If a tenant who has been in place for 17 years and paid all rents in excess of $2.8 million dollars in those years and has had NO breaches in their lease can be evicted, then new Sections are needed in the Commercial Tenancy Act that enable the tenant a first right of refusal, especially if the lease is connected to a business that is a means of livelihood for the people who own that business. Leaving decisions up to one or two people in leasing who may or may not feel like leasing a space to a tenant is just leaving holes open for bribery, scams, fraud, evicting without cause, and unethical business practices. Situations similar to what Bobby Dazzler experienced are common but many small retailers have not been able to expose the unethical practice until now. This means that even leases can essentially lead down the same road as political corruption and shady dealings that make the large larger and shut the small out. Sadly, that is what really needs to be transformed in order for diverse, small, independent retailers to survive and thrive in the retail transformation.

Without getting into the laws and rules for each state or country, it is important to note that there is definitely an underlying problem. Unethical business practices do exist and the large mimic the large. It is hard not to notice how the large business and chains dominated the malls with their presence, but they also are the ones leaving the biggest holes in retail space when they fall. The small retailers that offered unique shopping experiences along with unique products have been pushed out to street level or strip malls by the larger landlords. Those smaller retailers that offer diversity would have been able to provide sustainability to the malls, as they usually offer a loyal following that ensures a "return" client and loyalty to the malls. Instead, malls were cookie-cut to be just like the next one offering the exact same wares. That is where the problems started as far this small, independent retailer is concerned. The final result is the demise of fun, cool and exciting retail, and blasé retail in its place.

EPILOGUE

Like any new store or new business opening, Bobby Dazzler had passion, excitement and was eager for our business to launch back in 1990. It was an epic moment for any retailer whose life-long dream was to do just that. All the events that lined up the right ducks made that dream possible for almost 30 years. Retailing for that long can make one an "industry expert". A background to retailing was provided so that an up and coming retailer is able to see what type of foundation may be necessary. Vision is without a doubt is the best gift for the retail world. Bobby Dazzler attempted to show the reader that like all businesses, ups and downs are all part of the retail world. A personal and rare glimpse into the daily Bobby Dazzler retail world revealed that so many aspects of business need to be considered to operate smoothly. Retailing is challenging. Business is challenging everyday. There are many highs of profits, and downs that are sometimes related to the economy while in other instances, the problems are related to doing business with the wrong people. But these are all learning curves that are meant to be shared.

Retailing has come a long way since 1990. Retail in the past was simple, basic and easy to run with very little to worry about other than the local competitor. During the early days, retailing was much easier when it was just bricks and mortar stores that operated without much influence from the outside world of online retailers. Sure, there was catalog shopping and mail order but the information age drastically changed the way customers buy their stuff. It is a complex retail world that the digital age along with the use of technology we deal with daily. The whole world now is able to compete with all the retailers of the world.

Bobby Dazzler attempted to provide a glimpse into the "how to" aspects of retailing by introducing the reader to the kind of knowledge, background and skills which are necessary to lay the foundations to launch a retail store. Retailing can be a fun, exciting and profitable business if run with the right tools and background information. Bobby Dazzler attempted to provide a base for up-and-coming retailers to learn from and to build upon if a transformation is to take place. This information was meant to be very informative for retailers and customers who may be examining retail as a possible career choice or those who are just interested in finding out what retailing was like for a small, mom and pop business.

Bobby Dazzler felt that everything that happened, happened right at the store. It was an action filled memoir which had a plot thickening each and every day, an attempt to "reveal all" as to what happened over the years. The people, the clients, the pests, the bully and the owner (landlord), the large organizations are all part of the retail story of Bobby Dazzler. Bobby Dazzler felt that revealing the personal challenges in an authentic manner based on memory was essential for the reader to understand that these situations do happen. Bobby Dazzler always felt as if an injustice had taken place back in 2007 and it was necessary to speak up about it. Additionally, the abusive nature of the personal experiences needed to be revealed in a "whistle blowing" manner as nothing had come about after so many complaints. Enough was enough!

Bobby Dazzler was also able to provide a detailed examination of many issues, challenges and hurdles that ALL retailers face each day. There are many people in the retail world that need to be kept happy in order for a retailer to run smoothly. Factors such as online shopping, buyer behavior/habits, the effects of ganja, the high cost of everything and all the external factors that make the retail world go through so many changes, is the whole point of the story behind Bobby Dazzler. Sure, small retail is able to adapt better than the large but some of the large problems that Bobby Dazzler faced personally were simply too daunting to ever consider going back into retail again. Bobby Dazzler was part of the retail world for a long time and it was also part of the apocalypse of 2017 that went into 2018. After all, if it was profitable, we would still keep going. Bobby Dazzler just didn't think that a massive turnaround was immanent. So, we had NO reluctance when we closed our doors in the middle of the apocalypse in order to avoid any major personal financial disasters. Without any liabilities and with a very large donation of our final inventory to Surrey Christmas bureau and the Surrey School District for vulnerable teens, we felt that we done all that could have been done in our days as a retailer. We always had the vision to write about our retail secrets. It was exciting to share and it made it so much easier to close that retail chapter of our lives. Writing brought a final closure to something that was life itself for Bobby Dazzler. Retailing is based heavily on the materialistic world. The collapse of some 8,640+ stores by mid-2017 and more in 2018 may be a sign for humanity to perhaps search for something bigger than the retail world. This retail apocalypse may just lead to humanity choosing to shift its focus to more meaningful spiritual experiences rather than in the collection of more "stuff" to fill their homes with

After all, when the retailer door closed, another opened up as a healer for this business. That would be the next journey for Bobby Dazzler.

ABOUT THE AUTHOR

Bobby Dazzler was a pseudonym used by the author Jasbir Rai to write this "reveal all" retail book. Bobby Dazzler was a local British Columbian retailer who had been a leader in the industry for nearly 30 years. Bobby Dazzler was a strong, local strategic retailer that was able to last many years in a field that is notorious for many ups and downs. It was time to speak up about the abusive nature of large organizations. Small retail is not able to survive nor thrive due some very significant bullying that took place. Sharing this experience may seem like whistle blowing. However, the truth does need to be revealed so that others can also learn and be helped to under stand just how the struggle was in the retail world for this small retailer.

After going through many general and personal challenges including experiencing the retail apocalypse first hand, a time had come for this retailer to change directions and become a healer. After dealing with humanity on a material level, there was a self discovery that evolved from the struggles, the problems and all the adversity that was experienced which would lead this retailer choosing another path that was much more aligned to the soul purpose. In the meantime, a wonderful personal story had been created that was meant to be shared for many to enjoy about this small, local independent retailer who lasted so long in the challenging retail world. This experience, essentially acted as a catalyst for the next manuscript on spirituality, now published as *G-D's Eye: Universal Awakening*.

Bobby Dazzler closed its retail doors in June 2017, Jasbir Rai has been pursuing personal spiritual growth and raising her two teens in West Vancouver, BC. She enjoys writing and learning. (BA, 1996, Simon Fraser University and Certificate in Liberal Arts, 1993, SFU)

More info at www.bobbydazzler.ca

Also by Bobby Dazzler: *G-D's Eye: Universal Awakening*

Made in the USA
Middletown, DE
13 September 2018